This book is dedicated to you,
my new rich friend.

In loving memory of
Ella James, my forever supporter.

Money In Your Twenties: The Financial Workbook for The Young, Rich & Responsible

The content of this book is intended for educational and informational purposes only. It's designed to provide you with insights and strategies to enhance your understanding of personal finance. The author of this book is a financial educator, not a licensed financial advisor or legal professional. The information and advice provided herein are not meant to substitute professional financial or legal advice. Each individual's financial situation is unique. While the tips and strategies shared in this book are crafted with care, they may not be suitable for everyone. You are encouraged to consider your personal financial circumstances and, where appropriate, seek advice from qualified professionals before making any concrete financial decisions. Financial success is influenced by various factors, including individual effort, market conditions, and personal circumstances. Therefore, the author and publisher do not guarantee any specific financial outcome as a result of applying the information in this book.

This paperback edition first published in 2024

Design by Isis Paynter
Cover Design by Deanna Bains

IBSN 979-8-9908986-0-8 (paperback)
IBSN 979-8-9908986-1-5 (ebook)

Published by Boujie Budgets, LLC
www.boujiebudgets.com

TABLE OF CONTENTS

INTRODUCTION
Money is Hard

The vacation FINALLY made it out of the group chat. You're on the beach sipping your fifth Paloma on your last day in paradise. You've been working hard for the last couple of months, and it feels good to enjoy your money. Soaking in the beachy breeze in your temporary reality, you remember that in the next 24 hours, you'll be back on a plane to your real life. Back to work, home, and all the adulting things you must do to afford your next vacation.

You finally return home, and a gloomy, dark cloud starts forming. It's not the clouds outside; this gloom is in the pit of your stomach because you need to check your bank account post-paradise. There was no vacation budget, just vibes. And now you're about to pay for it, literally.

This scenario is an unfortunate reality for many people. You aren't alone if you've been there before, but please know you should never feel on edge when thinking about your finances. When you think about your money, you should feel excited and empowered. I'm sure that's why you decided to pick up this book. You're tired of feeling naive, broke, and uncomfortable.

I've been there. I did everything by the book. I did exactly what they told me to do: go to college (rack up student loans), get a good internship, and use the good internship to get a good job so I could live happily ever after. Right?!

Wrong, so, so very wrong. In the first three months of working my good big girl job, I had blown my $5,000 bonus, and to this day, I can't tell you what I spent the money on. I stared at my credit card statement and knew something needed to change. But I had no idea where to start.

In the YouTube search bar, I typed, "How to start a simple budget." Don't judge me; I'm a Zillennial (too old for Gen Z, too young for Millennials). Every question I have can be answered on YouTube, or so I thought. Video after video revealed that was not the case. They were all the same: some bored housewife with two kids, a dog, and a husband who made $150K for the family or an extreme money nerd who sold all their belongings, biked 20 miles to and from work, and only ate rice and beans. You know, the type who never went out with friends because their idea of fun was clipping coupons.

No, thank you.

1

I knew immediately that would NEVER be me. I didn't dream of a life where all the fun was sucked from the air with a heavy-duty vacuum. I wanted to live a rich life and have fun. I wasn't planning for kids, marriage, or buying a house. To be honest, I was still blowing money at the bar, partying every weekend, and trying to decide which Caribbean Island the girls and I were going to next. I knew there had to be a better way for me to budget. There had to be a way to create a life I truly enjoyed without sacrificing fun in my 20s.

So, I created the Flexible Budget™.

It took me about six months to perfect the Flexible Budget™. Luckily, thanks to this finance workbook, you'll learn the method in a fraction of that time.

If you're reading this, you have officially started a new chapter in your money story! I am proud of you. I also thank you for trusting me to lead you through this new journey. I know that money is a touchy topic, but the reality is that we need it to survive. This workbook was designed to help you better budget your money and take control of your life. Remember, your 20s are for fun, mistakes, and building your wealth foundation.

I'm taking you through my proven budgeting framework to get you started on the right path to wealth. This is not just a budgeting workbook; it's the foundation of your financial future.

You will have clear action steps to complete at the end of each section. Do not skip them. If you ever feel overwhelmed or uncomfortable, that means the change is happening; don't fight it.

Who This Book Is For

I wrote this book for everyone who feels like money and budgeting have never worked for them—for the people who did everything "right" yet still feel like something's missing. This book is for people who were never taught the simple things about money and who are struggling to transition into adulthood because of it.

If you've ever asked yourself, "Why didn't anyone teach me about money?" this is the book for you. If you've tried to get your money together but felt overwhelmed by all the conflicting advice online, this workbook was created with you in mind. If you're tired of all the "hacks" and ready to create a thoughtful money system to reach your financial goals, keep reading. If you've tried other budgeting techniques that didn't feel right for you and your lifestyle, it is my hope that this book will guide you and help you create a budget you can actually stick to.

This is for my first-generation college graduates who are the breadwinners in their families and need to figure this money thing out for themselves and the families depending on them. This book is your reminder that you are not alone. Your mistakes do not define who you are.

This book is a friendly money conversation. It is a guided workbook to help you think, but most importantly, ACT. The sole purpose of this book is to provide you with tangible action steps to create a financial foundation that will bring more money, more confidence, and more opportunities. The fact you chose this book proves you're ready for more. This is a book designed for action, and it was created with you in mind—from one friend to another.

Why You Need to Budget

My budget literally resembled a bad report card, so I created the Flexible Budget™ to take the shame out of spending.

Warning: **BUDGETS ONLY WORK IF YOU WORK WITH THEM.**

Before we jump into the Flexible Budget™, let me share some guided tips to help prepare you for the journey.

I developed a straight-to-the-point budgeting framework because I was tired of seeing lengthy budget templates (I am an accountant, but only at work). Traditional budgeting never seemed realistic to me. When I allocated the old way, I would just make up random numbers that sounded right for each line item. Then, at the end of the month, I was STILL overspending in almost every category. It felt like I was failing myself every month. I needed a budget that helped me win!

Let's Get Started!

Applying what you learn in this workbook and setting up the right financial systems will change you for the better. You (or someone who wants you to win) purchased this workbook to help you and your finances improve. So, take it seriously; I dare you.

Remember, this guide was designed with you in mind, so be honest with yourself about your money. Lying will only cheat you.

How to Use This Book

This is a workbook AND a reference book whose sole intention is to help you learn and take action. It was designed so you can easily refer back to specific sections for a refresher whenever necessary. Each section of this workbook includes some key features to add more clarity and context and to get you working on your money foundation. Read it once, read it twice, and then read it again when you have a money question and need a little guidance.

This workbook is best for those who have a consistent salary-based income, HOWEVER if you are paid hourly or part of the gig economy you can still get lots of value from this book. There may be a few tweaks needed to set up your Flexible Budget™.

Section Objectives: The boring yet important stuff. The section objectives give you a quick preview of what you will learn in each section so you have some context before diving into the topic.

Why Should You Care?: This is for the people who asked, "When am I ever going to use this?" or "What does this have to do with anything?" in school. Before you get started, you will know exactly why the section was added to this workbook and why it's important for you to know.

Rich Tips: These are extra pieces of advice to help you along the way. This workbook is flooded with random Rich Tips, giving you even more financial guidance for each section topic.

Act Rich, Be Responsible Exercises: This is a workbook, so yes, you have to do them. Each exercise is designed to keep you engaged and reinforce all the new money lessons you learn. Exercises are marked and have instructions to help you complete them.

Section Key Points: Quick refresher points at the end of each section to remind you of the most important information. These are easy reference points when you need a little reminder.

Reflection Questions: Not only will this workbook help you work on new money systems, but it will also encourage you to reflect on your past, present, and future. Each section ends with two reflection questions related to the section information.

Self-Assessment

Your first exercise is a self-reflection one. Addressing your money means taking responsibility and giving yourself a good, hard look in the mirror. You will be able to take another self-assessment after you've completed all the exercises in this workbook. For now, the most important action you can take is being honest with yourself. Be honest about how you feel about yourself and your money. Honesty and transparency are how you will grow. No one will see these answers, so no one can judge you in this space.

Act Rich, Be Responsible

EXERCISE #1:
Self Assessment

Instructions:

For each statement below, rate yourself on a scale of 1 to 10 (with 10 being completely agree) based on how much the statement reflects your current feelings. This will help you understand where your money mindset is today.

I feel confident in my ability to make strategic money decisions.

1   2   3   4   5   6   7   8   9   10

I feel confident in my ability to increase my current income.

1   2   3   4   5   6   7   8   9   10

I feel confident in my ability to manage the money I make.

1   2   3   4   5   6   7   8   9   10

I feel confident in my ability to achieve my current money goals.

1   2   3   4   5   6   7   8   9   10

I feel like I have a safe space to ask tough money questions.

1   2   3   4   5   6   7   8   9   10

I feel like I am financially responsible.

1   2   3   4   5   6   7   8   9   10

I feel confident in my power to change my current financial situation.

1   2   3   4   5   6   7   8   9   10

CHANGE YOUR MONEY MINDSET

SECTION OBJECTIVES

1. Address your past, present, and future relationship with money.

2. Create intentions to begin your budgeting journey.

3. Practice gratitude for your current financial life.

WHY SHOULD YOU CARE?

Start in a Safe Space: Creating a safe and happy place is the best way to begin your financial journey.

Uncover Money Blocks: Addressing the inner voice stopping you from reaching your full potential sets you up for success.

Reduces Stress and Anxiety: A positive mindset can help reduce stress and anxiety associated with budgeting and empower you to approach the process with a sense of optimism and confidence.

Your Mindset is Your Superpower

Some superheroes can fly, others have super strength. One thing all superheroes have in common is that they believe. They believe in their powers; they believe they can save lives, and because they believe, they do it.

The way you think about your money influences how you show up and interact with your dollars. Simply put, your mindset will either be your super strength or your kryptonite.

There will be obstacles with every new financial level you unlock. The roadblocks that lie ahead are why having a positive money mindset is truly important.

You will have to constantly remind yourself that mistakes are temporary. What I love most about money is that it's one of the few things in life that you can mess up and still recover from. Your recovery time, however, depends on your ability to see the silver lining through the cloudy mistakes of your past, present, and future. Friend, your mindset is your superpower.

Who Told You About Money?

Everything you know about money, you learned from the adults around you growing up, even if you claim you never learned anything about it. Growing up, you watched how the adults in your life interacted with the world. You listened to how they talked about money. You internalized how their money habits impacted you.

As you grew into adulthood, all those quiet money lessons started to resurface. You started replaying those messages from the years in your head. In your 20s, there are conversations about money everywhere you turn: on social media when people announce huge purchases like cars and homes, amongst your friends as you start paying real bills and building new relationships, with coworkers when you notice them taking their PTO...and how nice your manager's car is. We're always thinking about money, but for some reason, no one is talking about it.

Think about who you talk to about money. Are you in community with friends who are open with you about their salary, expenses, and investments? Do you have mentors and older adults who give you insight into your tough money questions? Have you had open and honest money conversations with your romantic partner?

If you don't have safe spaces to talk about money, now is the time to create them. You don't have to start screaming your salary from the rooftops, but you can begin talking to your community about this amazing financial workbook you just started reading and share interesting money videos in the group chat. Your conversations can begin evolving to include topics such as investing, salaries, and other major money moves. Then, you'll begin to level up and find more folks who are willing to have those conversations too.

Ghosts of Money Trauma's Past

Our past has a unique way of showing up out of thin air in our everyday lives. Money traumas are shaped by major events and experiences. Whether it's growing up in poverty, amassing thousands of dollars in debt, or generational trauma passed down, financial trauma is very real. How we use money is a combination of how we feel when we have it and how we feel when it's gone. We are in a constant state of learning when it comes to money. Your collective memories and experiences determine what gets spent, what gets saved, and everything in between.

Our money ghosts love to haunt us, but just like the ghosts in movies, most people never even see them. "Money gurus" will tell you it's necessary to separate money from emotions. But this just isn't true or possible unless you're a human cyborg with no sensory feelings. Since you're probably not a cyborg, there's a good chance a money ghost is following you, carrying your money traumas. Common money trauma responses are overspending, underspending, or avoidance. Pay attention not only to how you spend but also when you spend.

When You Spend: Most people only think of the "How" when it comes to spending. One of the most impactful books I've read in my life was *When* by Daniel Pink. The power of when something happens can make all the difference.

Fun fact: people with the number 9 at the end of their age are more likely to run their first marathon. Think 29, 39, 49, 59—these people probably set a goal to do a marathon before the next "big age" milestone.

When you spend can be ruled by your money ghost, just as much as how much you spend. People who tend to procrastinate, like me, are usually those who spend more money at the end of the month. People who tend to be anxious often spend more money at the beginning of the month. Going to college near a major Naval base, it was always obvious when it was the 1st or the 15th of the month because the soldiers would be seen spending like there was no tomorrow.

Overspending: My momma is a shopaholic. Growing up in a home with a chronic overspender made me hate spending money. Well, because of her childhood, her money ghost probably told her to create a space where she could spend freely. Now? She doesn't even need a reason to buy things other than she saw it, she liked it, and she bought it. Her story is not unique, but overspending can be a response to other traumas as well.

Do you remember how it felt when you couldn't get the thing you really wanted? Can you recall a time when it became painfully obvious that your family didn't have as much money as one of your friends? Your money ghost can. They've been holding onto those emotions, collecting all the experiences that made you feel that way. When you finally got that good job or came up on the money you needed, your ghost probably whispered, "Ball out!"

When we were in college, we used to talk about the things we'd do when we finally got the big corporate check. Fixing my teeth was always my plan; the hatred for my not-quite-straight teeth and memories of getting bullied for the size of my two front teeth were the motivation.

The question is as old as time, "What would you do if you won the lottery?" We all dream about spending money or having enough to spend freely without fear of ending up broke.

Your ghost might convince you to be a different kind of overspender. Maybe your money ghost is constantly comparing you to an old college classmate who seems to be able to afford the vacation you want. That voice in the back of your head saying, "Spend it, you gon' get it right back," is the work of your nasty money ghost. Sometimes, your money ghost is so comfortable with you living paycheck to paycheck that they encourage you to overspend, securing their comfortable spot and ensuring they live to survive another day. Your money ghost is afraid of you. They're terrified that you might wake up one day and realize they're as fake as a $3 bill because then they won't be able to control you or your money, and without you, they die.

Underspending: Do you know what happens when a shopaholic and an underspender get married? They birth a financial educator! My parents are the definition of yin and yang in many ways, especially when it comes to how they view money. No two money ghosts are created the same; some ghosts are extreme cheapskates. My dad is the second oldest of five children, and, like my momma, he grew up in a house with a single mother. Unlike my momma, my dad hates spending money. Growing up, he was what I call a "waste not". If there were leftovers, he ate them. If someone was giving away clothes, he'd make them fit. If it was second-hand, his hands were where it went. If my dad had a catchphrase, it would be, "If it's free, it's for me."

Some people have a money ghost who's convinced them to save every dollar because cheaper is better, and a dollar saved is a dollar earned. Their ghost probably remembers times when they didn't have control over their money, so now, the only way to keep their ghost from nagging is to go with the cheaper option. Their ghost thrives on clipping every coupon known to man and makes decisions based solely on price, nothing else.

When was the last time your ghost persuaded you to do a DIY project? I'm convinced that the people who DIY everything so they can save a little money have money ghosts who are control freaks. I know you know the type—the people who swear their at-home drip coffee is so much better than Starbucks because the thought of spending more money than necessary makes their money ghost moan so loud they get chills.

Does your money ghost thrive on experiences that prove it's unsafe to spend money or bully you into cutting corners because cheaper is better? The truth is your ghost doesn't care about your mental and physical health—they only care that you pay the least amount of money possible.

Money Avoidance: If you're the person who chooses to take a nap when you have a to-do list longer than the Nile River, you know a thing or two about avoiding your responsibilities. If you tend to avoid the big stuff, this has probably shown up in your money too. Avoidance might look like opting out of checking your bank accounts, neglecting past-due payments, or not mentioning money in any way.

Reality check: avoiding your money issues won't make them go away or get better. If anything, avoiding your money issues will make them go from bad to worse. You're not doing yourself any favors neglecting your finances. In fact, your money ghost gets stronger every day you choose avoidance. To kill your money-avoidance ghost, you need to shed light on your mistakes, own up to them, and quit napping on the job.

Act Rich, Be Responsible

EXERCISE #2:
Fill in the Blank

Instructions:
Read through the paragraph and fill in the blanks without hesitation. If you can't come up with a word, look at your surroundings, find an object, and think of word associations for that object. An example is below.

Money has always been a source of <u>**CONFUSION**</u> for me. From a young age, I learned about money from my family, particularly <u>**HOW TO SPEND MONEY**</u>. These experiences have shaped my relationship with finances, and I can see how they've influenced my financial decisions. One specific memory that stands out is when <u>**I COULDN'T AFFORD SCHOOL LUNCH.**</u> That made me feel <u>**EMBARRASSED**</u>. Looking back, I can see how this experience has contributed to my current money mindset. To release these limitations and move toward financial abundance, I need to confront these old beliefs and replace them with new ones, such as <u>**BELIEVING MONEY IS ABUNDANT.**</u> This will help me achieve my financial goals and create a healthier relationship with money.

> **Reflect on your relationship with your money out loud. What does money mean to you?**

> **Growing up, what was your experience with money? What did your family teach you about finances?**

In my life, money has always represented_____. Whenever I think about money, I feel_____. This feeling stems from my earliest memories of money, particularly when_____.
One recurring thought I have about money is_____. This thought often leads me to take actions like_____. However, I now realize that this thought may be holding me back because_____.
To address this, I commit to exploring my beliefs about money and its impact on my life, and I will work on changing these patterns by_____.

What are some external forces that impact your current financial habits?

Reflecting on your childhood, how did the adults in your life feel about money? What words and phrases did they use when talking about money?

What is the happiest money memory you have? What did you do with your money, and what emotions do you think of?

In order to explore my relationship with money, I first need to acknowledge my_____
_____. These beliefs have been ingrained in me since_____. To uncover the hidden thoughts that influence my financial decisions, I must confront my fear of _____. It's important to recognize that these mental blocks have been holding me back from achieving my financial goals. To release these limitations, I will start _____. By shining a light on these blocks, I can begin the journey toward a healthier and more prosperous financial future.

What current thoughts and feelings are holding you back from creating the financial future you dream of?

What are some thoughts and emotions that make you feel anxious or overwhelmed about your financial future?

When you think about your financial future what excites you?

MONEY AFFIRMATIONS TO KEEP YOU MOTIVATED

I deserve the money I receive for my work

I am capable of creating my life exactly as I want it to be

My Money has a positive impact on my life

My Money is the root of all things wonderful

My Money is a tool to help me achieve my goals

I am in control of my money and finances

I am worthy of being financially secure

I deserve luxurious goods, services, and experiences

Money is of abundance and all around me

I am a powerful money magnet

Act Rich, Be Responsible

EXERCISE #3:
Gratitude List

Instructions:

Set a timer for five minutes and list all the things you are grateful for in your life. Think of everything that brings you health, wealth, love, and peace. Small things and little things can be included in this list.

Act Rich, Be Responsible

EXERCISE #4:
Intentional Wordsearch

Instructions:

In the word search below, find the first three words that set the intention for the next phase of your money journey. Then, write a statement of intention using the words you found.

```
O L X M H B R Z U M L I M I T L E S S H D U K H Z L D Z X J
S T A B I L I T Y S D D E S E R V E M Z F A D Z F C P T J X
P O E E H Y D B N F V F Q I N T E G R I T Y O C F L C D K H
H R A L K Y N U K G R A T E F U L U F U L F I L L A S F F X
Q G K E M I W D O R Z R U G K M G R O W T H N N E J C N F X
E A X V T W L G M A G P T F Y Z Z I R E S P O N S I B L E R
S N H A S I X E O T L E F R F S M A R T C L A R I T Y V O H
S I E T V U D T N I W A P R O D U C T I V E M H W F J X K X
U Z V E I H U Z E T I C O V E R F L O W I N G O P J G R M S
C E O Y H W M O Y U E E D B P S B D B E L I E V E D D Q P P
C D L S B O O F P D R Z E R U V U W C Z D I L I G E N T F R
E Z V C O N F I D E N C E J R L P Z O G P E E G H J X P O O
S Q E Y L K L C Y G Y C W P P W B S M R K V O D C L Q M Q C
S H S S A V I N G S P F S B O R M T M A N R O Q Q W K M R E
F F V B N M G E N E R O U S S X N C I C U I X G J E H D U S
L A B U N D A N C E Y N W Y E Y D P T E G C Y B I A U J K S
L D W Q D A G R M R M I N D F U L R M P K H R I Q L U Y R L
N Z R I G S C C E M P O W E R E D O E P K N W W H T W V E Y
B Y R I F L H S H A Q F O O Q C I G N W H V A C D H A F W H
T P O N A H Z S F V F S R B T Q S R T U Z B Q D T T U I A P
H R C C V E C I X J E A T I R X C E V I C T O R I O U S R R
R I C R S M B M Z S A F H W U H I S R S F V B O Q G K N D E
I O I E U P B P H R R E Y Z S P P S N U K R J V O M I E I P
V R X A H E E L G X L T L X T L L D V G Z R L N A U N N N A
I I G S C B C I I M E Y H B L U I W B T Y S K F U U D V G R
N T T E A D R C Y W S Z D B O P N T T G B F B Z V L N L Q E
G Y Y W E N P I U O S A J U C V E B O V K R V T E C E N B D
L T N F F I H T S I I N V E S T M E N T Z T N T M P S U S Y
P B H F N G K Y G W H Q U Z X L P S L F J V I W H Y S X M E
V W E A X N F P E R S I S T E N T W X B U E D E D D H S J R
```

Word #1

Word #2

Word #3

Intention Statement 1

Intention Statement 2

Intention Statement 3

Section Notes

CREATING GOALS THAT STICK

SECTION OBJECTIVES

1. Learn the importance of mindset shifts to transform your finances.

2. Create strong financial goals to win in any season of your life.

3. Establish an action plan for success.

WHY SHOULD YOU CARE?

🪙 **Clarity and Focus:** Developing a focused mindset and setting clear goals are essential prerequisites to effective budgeting.

🪙 **Motivation and Persistence:** Budgeting requires discipline and perseverance, especially when faced with temptations or unexpected setbacks.

🪙 **Builds Organizational Skills:** Setting intentional goals helps to form and organize your money system.

Forgiving Yourself

You have been sold a lie. The lie in question is that budgeting is the first step toward financial freedom. This couldn't be further from the truth. The real first step to financial freedom is getting your mindset right. This looks like identifying your habits, creating goals, and, most importantly, forgiving yourself.

I know you picked up this budgeting workbook expecting to get right into the numbers. But the truth is, numbers mean nothing if there isn't a story behind them. As the Boomers say, "You can lead a horse to water, but you can't make 'em drink." I can give you every money hack and budgeting framework I can think of, but it will be a waste of time (and this book) if you haven't done the necessary mental work. You need to truly believe that your financial situation will get better, and forgiveness is the only way to put out your burning fire of negativity.

The mistakes you made in the past do not define who you are. Bad money decisions are a result of financial traumas, negative financial influences, and a lack of financial literacy, not a reflection of who you are.

Do what you need to truly forgive yourself. Write a letter. Give yourself a pep talk in the mirror. Tweet it into existence. Whatever you need to do to let that hurt go, do it.

You cannot change the past, but you can acknowledge and learn from it. It's only up from here.

Act Rich, Be Responsible

EXERCISE #5:
Forgiving Yourself

Instructions:

In the space below, write a letter of forgiveness to your past self. Think of your past money mistakes, acknowledge them as the mistakes they are, and create space for forgiveness.

A Letter of Forgivness to Yourself

Sticky Goals

Directly after forgiveness comes setting your goals for your future success. It's time to get serious about your money. You cannot build a solid money system without goals to work toward. You are destined for success, but without goals, your system is broken before you even start.

Your goals should be strong and sticky. I'm not talking about Elmer's Glue sticky; I'm talking about Gorilla Glue sticky.

Handwritten goals are more likely to stick. So, write your goals down and watch the work start (there is no magic, just hard work).

Your goals need to be SMART. SMART goals are Specific, Measurable, Attainable, Relevant, and Time-Based. I personally like to add a "Why" statement to my goals, making my SMART goals SMARTY.

Your "why" is your driving point. It's why you need to hit your money goal and how it will help improve your life. Your why statement gives your goals purpose.

On the next page is an example of one goal shown in two different ways: loose and sticky. Pay attention to the differences. Use the example as inspiration to fuel your ideas for your new money goals. The SMARTY method is a great way to focus on the details of your goals and get your brain excited for new challenges.

SMARTY Goal Example

	Loose	Sticky
S Specific	I am going to save some money	I am going to save $10,000
M Measurable	I will see more money saved	I will track the money in my savings account every week
A Attainable	I will save money every month	I will use this workbook to set up automatic savings to hit my goals
R Relevant	Even though I have nothing ($0.00) saved, I need more money in the bank	I have control over my money and this goal will help me be a finacially savvy person
T Time-based	I want to have more money this year	In 12 months, I will save $10,000 in my emergency fund account
Y Why	To have more money in the bank	I need to create a safety net to start my investing portfolio

Plan of Action

Goals are useless without a plan of action. James Clear wrote, "Winners and losers have the same goals." What sets winners apart from losers are the different systems and action plans they put in place to help them win. It's not enough to write a nice-sounding goal. You have to adjust your habits to get to your desired level of success.

Creating a system for success gives you the habits of a winner. It's not just about waking up at 5am every day and doing a two-hour morning routine. Habits are autopilot functions that can be rewired and updated anytime. Identifying habits such as when you spend money, what you spend money on, and how you interact with your money will be your strongest asset to success.

Your action plan will become your habits, and your habits will bring you closer to your goals.

Rarely do we talk about how our habits play a huge role in our success. This book will give you the blueprint, but it's just a guide. You must be the driving force. You must believe in your ability and then commit to new actions and habits to reach your goals. If you skip one part of this foundation, then you might as well throw this book away because the change you're expecting will never come.

Keep your goals sticky and simple. Far too often, beginners get excited and try to set several goals at once. This is the fastest way to burn out and get overwhelmed. Change needs to happen gradually for it to truly be effective. My advice is no more than three goals for a twelve-month period. One goal focused on income (e.g., salary or side hustles). One goal focused on cash flow (e.g., debt payment). One goal focused on a money-related area of your finances (e.g., credit score).

After creating your sticky goals, it's time to create an action plan with milestones to keep you focused on hitting your goals. Think of your large goal as a four-legged chair. Each of the small legs ensures the chair is stable enough to hold you up.

Creating habits is key to staying focused and reaching your goals. Below is a sample of how you can create your own action items and habit commitments.

This Week's Action Items

Clear action items are the steps you take each week.

| open a high-yield saving account fun for my ATL move. | complete the finacial flow steps for my budget | Set up automatic transfers to my ATL move fund |

Goal: $10,000 in 12 months in my emergency fund.

Why:
To make me feel more financially stable in case of job loss or unexpected financial loss.

This Quarter's Money Habit Commitment

Habits are ongoing, actions are a one time thing.

Commitment 1: I commit to reviewing my bank accounts and spending,every payday at 8am.

Commitment 2: I commit to paying cash for all purchases under $10 or leaving it in the store.

Positive habits will help you stick to your budget.

23

Act Rich, Be Responsible

EXERCISE #6:
SMARTY Goals

Instructions:

Let's make a SMARTY Goal together. Answer the prompts below for ONE goal. Refer back to the Loose vs Sticky goal example to help you with this exercise.

What specific goal do you want to achieve?

How will you know have achieved your goal?

How can this be accomplished? List action steps.

How does this goal help your life?

When will this goal be completed? Set a target date.

What is the purpose of creating this goal?

Act Rich, Be Responsible

EXERCISE #7:
Action Plan

Instructions:
Write your action items for the next month and your habit commitment for the quarter. Use the Action Plan Example on page 23 for reference.

This Week's Action Items		
Action 1:	**Action 2:**	**Action 3:**

This Week's Action Items		
Action 1:	**Action 2:**	**Action 3:**

This Week's Action Items		
Action 1:	**Action 2:**	**Action 3:**

This Week's Action Items		
Action 1:	**Action 2:**	**Action 3:**

Section Key Points

🪙 Forgive yourself for past money mistakes and move on!

🪙 "Winners and losers have the same goals" you need a system for success.

🪙 You can't be a SMARTY without your "Y". Remember to create a why with every goal.

🪙 Keep it simple! You don't need more than three goals to focus on.

Write a statement of forgiveness to your future self. Give grace for the mistakes you have yet to make.

Describe what it will feel like to reach your financial goals. Be very descriptive.

Section Notes

ORGANIZING YOUR MONEY

SECTION OBJECTIVES

1. Understand your current money habits and weaknesses.

2. Categorize your finances with a budgeting allocation method.

3. Create a game plan for you to start spending with intention.

WHY SHOULD YOU CARE?

Financial Awareness and Control: Reviewing your spending habits and organizing your money provides a clear picture of your financial situation.

Prioritization: Identifying areas where you can cut back on expenses or redirect those funds toward your new financial goals will help you prioritize where and when you spend your money.

Building a Strong Financial Foundation: Reviewing your spending habits and establishing a budget is key to building a healthy financial future.

Budgeting Allocations

Now that you have a clear vision of where you want your relationship with money to go, it's time to review your past spending habits. The best way to evaluate your spending habits is to review your budget allocations. You do so by assessing how much of your total income is dedicated to a specific category. This will help you determine if you're spending too much money and see where it's going.

This exercise will reveal your spending gaps. Most people suggest a 50/30/20 allocation. Fifty percent (50%) of total income is allocated for needs, thirty percent (30%) of total income is allocated for wants, and twenty percent (20%) of total income is allocated for saving. There is *NOTHING* wrong with this allocation method.

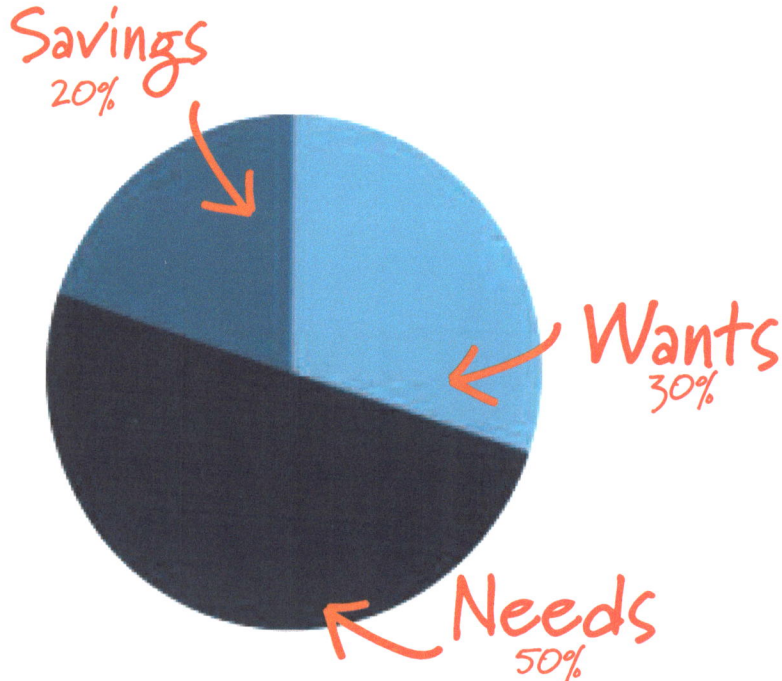

Savings
20%

Wants
30%

Needs
50%

Okay, so I lied when I said there's nothing wrong with the 50/30/20 rule. There is something wrong! This allocation method is extremely vague. Wants and needs are super subjective depending on who you are and what you do. So, let's clear it up.

Your budget should be flexible, but your allocations should be STIFF. The S.T.I.F.F Formula™ stands for Survive, Thrive, Invest, Fund, and Fun.

Survival represents your BASIC needs—the things you absolutely cannot survive without. Think food, water, medication, and shelter. You should allocate forty percent (40%) of your income to not dying.

Next, think about your "Thrive" expenses; these are the non-negotiable expenses that you need to thrive but not necessarily survive. Non-negotiables are normal expenses like your cell phone, Wi-Fi, and transportation. These line items are technically needs, but it's unclear whether these are wants or needs under the 50/30/20 rule. Make no mistake, I NEED my cell phone and Wi-Fi. You should allocate about twenty-five percent (25%) of your income to non-negotiables. Consider negotiating some of those bills to reduce prices (see page 71).

Investing is important whether you are interested in the stock market, real estate, fine goods, art collectibles, or digital assets. Investing NEEDS to be part of your budgeting allocation because this will be the way to grow your money faster. You will need to do your own research to find what ways of investing are most interesting to you, but focus on allocating 10% of your income to invest.

The first F is for Fund. Funding your savings should be 15% of your total income. Step Three of the Flexible Budget™ dives much deeper into savings, so I'll leave that for later, but for now, just remember, saving is paying your future self in the present.

Finally, the second F stands for Fun! You don't need these things to survive or thrive, but they make you happy. These are expenses that you can absolutely live without and can easily be cut off or scaled back without lowering your quality of life. Allocate 10% of your total income to your Fun.

That's the S.T.I.F.F Formula™! So, when you're reflecting on your budget, ask yourself, "How S.T.I.F.F are the rules for my money?"

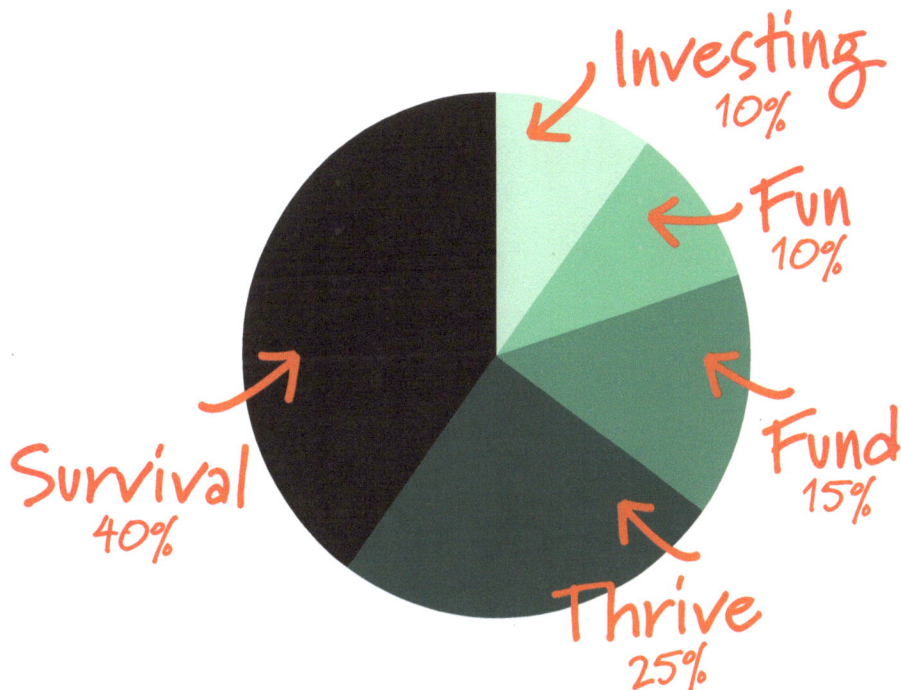

Investing 10%
Fun 10%
Fund 15%
Thrive 25%
Survival 40%

S.T.I.F.F Formula Breakdown

Survival	Thrive	Investing	Fund	Fun
Food (groceries) Rent/Utilities Medications *anything you need to not die	Phone Wi-Fi Transportation Music Streaming Debt Payment *anything you need to live comfortably	Stock Investing Real Estate Investing Mutual Funds ETFs Index Funds *anything that help your money work for you	Emergency Fund Retirement Fun Fund House Fund Travel Fund *goals for our future	Traveling Beauty/Grooming Dining Out/ Fast Food Clothing Entertainment Gym *extra happiness

The above grid includes some of my budget allocations. Keep in mind, depending on your lifestyle, your breakdown may vary. If you find your spending is outside of the recommended percentages, it may be time to scale back on your spending or increase your income.

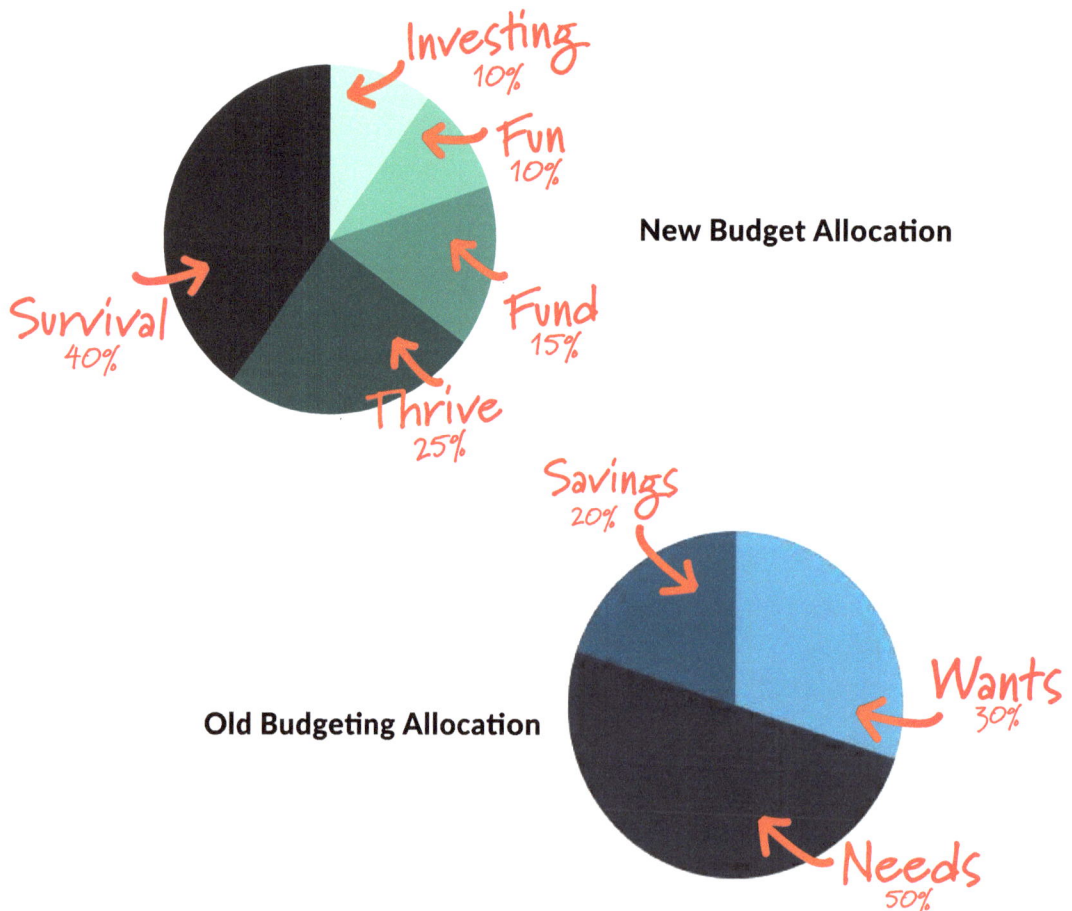

Investing
10%

Fun
10%

Fund
15%

Survival
40%

Thrive
25%

New Budget Allocation

Savings
20%

Wants
30%

Needs
50%

Old Budgeting Allocation

Reviewing Your Spending

Don't tell me what you care about. Show me your bank statements. Remember the habits we discussed in the last section?

In this section, you'll start uncovering your current habits by reviewing your past spending. You cannot make a plan for your path forward if you don't know what you're currently doing. When you are reviewing your bank statements, you should be looking for the following trends:

- When you are spending your money
- Where you are spending your money
- What accounts you are spending money from
- How much money you are spending
- Unfamiliar/Fraudulent transactions
- What subscriptions you have on auto-pay

Rich Tip: If you have multiple accounts and are unsure about what automatic payments are attached to each, cancel your cards. When it comes time to renew your subscription, they will notify you of a missed payment, and you can choose to keep or cancel your service then.

Tracking your spending will create space for you to "find" extra money and reallocate your spending to its new home in your revamped budget. This is not a habit you have to do every month, but it helps you be more intentional about how much you spend throughout the month. This is your money system; therefore, you choose how much effort you want to put into it. Digging through the past will make your future much brighter.

Before we go any further, I want to remind you to forgive yourself throughout this process. Yesterday's mistakes are today's lessons. It's hard to face your mistakes head-on, but you are ready for this. You have what it takes to change your current relationship with your money and make it a successful, loving one.

The problem most of us have is that we blindly spend money, but that stops today. This is the type of self-awareness that smacks you across the face and tells you, "There's food at home."

The only way to see your money mistakes is to track your spending.

Before you do this, repeat out loud, "I forgive myself for my past spending habits." Did you say it? Say it three more times. Seriously, forgive yourself before you even go down this rabbit hole. We have officially stepped into a new chapter, so leave that old baggage, hurt, and shame at the door. Now that you have forgiven yourself, let's get to work.

Budget Categories

Survive: Your BASIC needs you absolutely cannot physically live without (e.g., essential food, water, medications).

Thrive: The non-negotiable expenses that you need to have but can technically survive without (e.g., Wi-Fi, transportation, phone, debt payment).

Investing: Ways to have your money make more money for you (e.g., stock market, real estate, digital assets).

Fund: Savings for the future you (e.g., housing fund, emergency fund).

Fun: Negotiable expenses to help you live your best life (e.g., concerts, dining out, vacations)

Account Type

Spending Account: Any account(s) used for daily spending transactions (e.g., gas, hair, groceries, travel).

Savings Account: Any account(s) related to savings and not money meant to be spent immediately (e.g., IRA savings, certificate deposit, emergency savings, Christmas, vacation, house).

Bill Pay Account: Any account(s) used for recurring bills, most of which are the same amount from month to month (e.g., monthly subscriptions, rent, phone, Wi-Fi, credit card payments, loan payments).

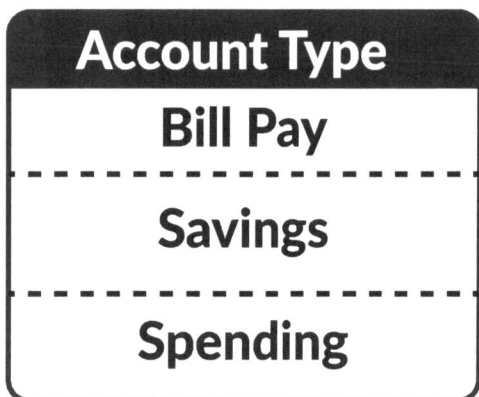

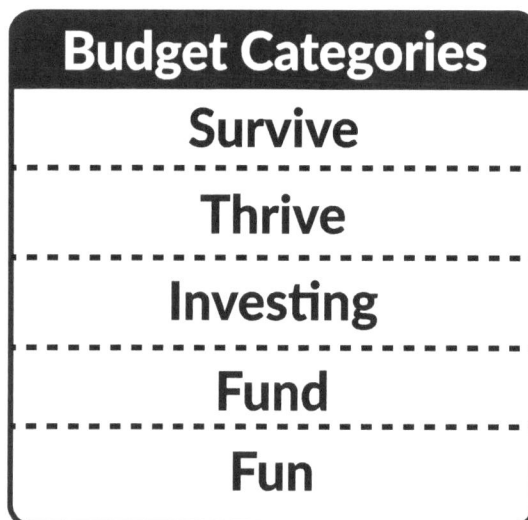

Account Type
Bill Pay
Savings
Spending

Budget Categories
Survive
Thrive
Investing
Fund
Fun

Act Rich, Be Responsible

EXERCISE #8:
Spending Audit

Instructions:

1. Download your personal bank and credit card statements from the last month.
2. Record all transactions and information in the tracker.
3. Calculate how much you spent in each category.
A few examples are done for you.

Disclaimer: This is probably the most difficult exercise in this entire workbook. It won't be fun, but it is very necessary. Set a timer for 10 minutes at a time and take breaks to ease any overwhelming feelings.

DATE	AMOUNT	TRANSACTION DESCRIPTION	BUDGET CATEGORY	ACCOUNT TYPE	BANK
11/09	$9.99	Tidal Music Payment	Thrive	Bill Pay	xyz bank
11/15	$150	Transfer to Emergency Fund	Fund	Savings	hysa bank
11/24	$43.79	Trader Joe's weekly grocery shopping	Survive	Spending	abc bank

DATE	AMOUNT	TRANSACTION DESCRIPTION	BUDGET CATEGORY	ACCOUNT TYPE	BANK

DATE	AMOUNT	TRANSACTION DESCRIPTION	BUDGET CATEGORY	ACCOUNT TYPE	BANK

Act Rich, Be Responsible

EXERCISE #9:
Budget Allocation

Instructions:

Organize your budget. Fill in the chart below with the expenses that should be included for each section of your budget allocation. Map out your current allocations in the circle below.

Survival	Thrive	Investing	Fund	Fun
*anything you need to not die	*anything you need to live comfortably	*anything that helps your money work for you	*goals for your future	*extra fun

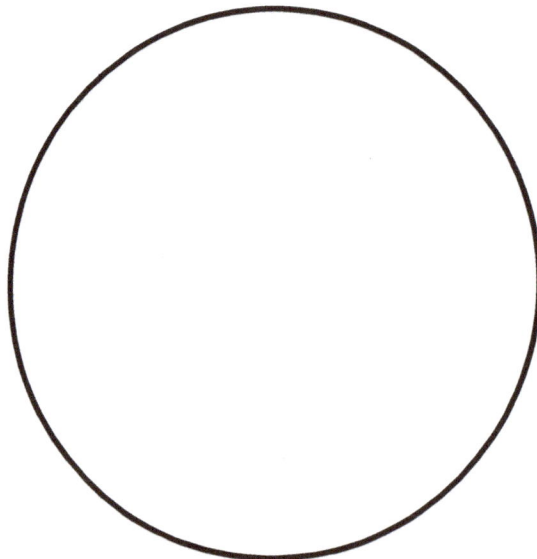

Current Spending Allocation

Section Key Points

- 🪙 Yesterday's mistakes are today's lessons.

- 🪙 Your bank statement will show you what you value and get you familiar with your spending habits.

- 🪙 Budgeting allocations guide your dollars and delegate your money to their respective and organized places.

- 🪙 Keep it simple! You don't need to overcomplicate it. The hardest part is done.

How do your current spending habits align with your financial goals and values? Identify one area where you could improve your spending.

Imagine you have successfully established a budgeting allocation method. Describe a specific situation where your budgeting method helped you make a more informed purchase decision.

Section Notes

SETTING UP YOUR MONEY SYSTEM

SECTION OBJECTIVES

1. Determine the bank accounts you need in your money system and understand how to use them.

2. Establish the tools and calculations required for automatic bill pay and savings within your money system.

3. Build your personal finance money system.

WHY SHOULD YOU CARE?

Protect Your Financial Well-being: Having a framework that helps you see how your money moves ensures that your finances are used strategically and in alignment with your long-term goals.

Streamline Financial Processes: Creating a system for your money is essential for organizing your finances and ensuring that you stay on track with your wealth-building goals.

Optimize Your Banking Experience: The right bank accounts will help with tracking your expenses, budgeting, and gaining insights into your spending patterns to support your financial decision-making.

Financial Technology (FinTech) was created to help make managing and growing your money easier. If you still rely on your mattress and snail-mailed checks to organize your money, I am judging you...harshly.

There are three important things you absolutely need to ensure you have an airtight money system:

1. The right bank accounts.
2. Perfectly calculated direct deposit.
3. Automatic bill payment.

The New Zero

The New Zero is your new "I'm Broke" limit.

Now, you probably look at your bank account when someone invites you out to determine whether or not you can afford to go. Most times, as long as your bank account isn't at a zero balance ($0.00), you wouldn't consider yourself broke. When your account hits a zero balance ($0.00), or worse, if your account is negative, this is when you recognize that you're actually broke.

The New Zero doesn't allow that reckless behavior. In short, **the New Zero is the lowest amount of money you will allow in your account at any given time.**

Personally, I keep AT LEAST one hundred dollars ($100) in every savings account I have. I'm not a millionaire (yet), so this is a very comfortable amount for me. However, **the more my wealth and income grow, the higher my zero will become.** I'm not comfortable with my bank account being at a zero balance ($0.00), and you shouldn't be either.

I determined my New Zero based on my monthly income, expenses, and debt level. Think of it this way: if your bank account had zero dollars, you wouldn't have any money to spend. Instead of a literal zero balance, you decide a new zero, or a new amount that would cause you to stop spending money. I'm that girl who will say, "I don't have the money," with $100-$200 sitting in my account.

Be that person! Train your brain to recognize your New Zero.

Turning on Notifications and Alerts

It's important to remember to set up bank alerts. Most mobile apps should give you the option to set spending alerts. Alerts can be in the form of emails, text messages, or push notifications. The method best for you will depend on how often you check it. If you're obsessed with your money like me, you'll have notifications for all three methods enabled!

Below is a checklist of alerts that should be set on each of your accounts:

- ☑ Withdrawls above $0.01
- ☑ Deposits above $0.01
- ☑ Savings balance drop below $100 (or your new zero)
- ☑ Weekly current balance

44

The Right Bank Accounts

Choosing a Bank Account

Before choosing a new bank, because I'm sure you will need one, review the bank's features. Any bank I choose and trust to hold my money needs four features. If a bank doesn't have all four of the following features, I REFUSE to give them my business. Here are my banking requirements:

- ☑ Online/mobile access
- ☑ No account minimums
- ☑ No hidden or overdraft fees
- ☑ Great customer service

Banks are notorious for hidden fees and low interest rates. I, for one, will not put up with it any longer, and neither should you. You need the right bank accounts. This means you are going to need multiple accounts at different institutions.

Have you heard the phrase, "Don't put all of your eggs in one basket"? Well, I'm hijacking it and telling you not to leave all of your money in one bank. This is for a couple of reasons.

One, the banking crash in 2008 exposed many institutions for the frauds they really are. You don't owe any financial company your loyalty; be loyal only to yourself and your money. These corporations already have billions.

Two, technology fails all the time. Companies get hacked, and systems go down. If all of your money is in one bank, you will be without access to your funds while they work out their tech issues.

The most your bank will likely do in this situation is email you an apology, but your landlord will still charge that late fee if you don't pay your rent on time. They won't care that it's your bank's fault. I suggest having a minimum of THREE different banking institutions to separate your money into.

Account One : Bill Pay Account

Bills must be paid first because that's how the world works. Your bill pay account should be in an easily accessible account. A national or large regional bank/credit union is best for the bill pay account because you and your creditors should have no problem accessing money transferred.

You will need to have a checking and savings account at this institution. Once you get your debit card, lock it up safely in your home and never take it out. The savings account will have a terrible interest rate, but that's where you'll keep your cushion money for variable expenses like utilities.

Account 2: High Yield Savings Account

If you don't have a savings account that provides at least a one percent (1%) return, it's time to rethink how you bank. The interest a savings account earns over the year depends on the rate. The higher the rate, the more free money you receive for allowing the bank to hold your funds. Always be mindful that you are the customer, and the bank needs you to sustain itself.

Opening a high-yield savings account was a game-changer for me. Some high-yield accounts offer an option to have a checking and savings account. Stick to only having a savings account to avoid having a way to easily spend money this is meant to be saved.

Rich Tip: Never attach a debit card to the high yield savings account.

The more difficult it is to access your savings, the more likely it is that you'll leave the money alone so it can be fruitful and multiply. If this is an online-only bank, you will need to transfer funds electronically from one of your other banks. This is one reason to keep those old brick-and-mortar banks around.

Account Three: Spending Account

The third and final bank account you need is one for your daily spending. The best bank for this is the one that works best with your spending habits and doesn't charge an overdraft fee or any other hidden fees. This bank shouldn't require a minimum to open and maintain the account. Only trash banks require a $25 minimum plus monthly maintenance fees.

Break up with any bank that doesn't respect you as a customer.

I recommend online banks without fees for spending because they give you space to make mistakes while you're getting your finances together. As a recovering unintentional spendaholic, you'll thank me for encouraging you to make this switch. You will make mistakes, but those moments of overspending should never cost you an extra $36.50 in addition to the negative balance you may have.

Once you have the right accounts, it's time to fund them with the right amount of money. The next step is to calculate the exact amount required for direct deposit.

Rich Tip: Some new FinTech companies have rebranded account maintenance fees and now call them "subscription" fees. These are the same concept. Do not pay a bank for holding your money... ever. Look out for those sneaky terms when signing up for new FinTech companies.

What about Credit Unions?

Credit unions are kinda like banks but with a friendlier vibe. Imagine your local community coming together to create a financial institution that's all about helping each other out. That's a credit union!

Instead of being owned by big shareholders or investors, credit unions are owned by the members themselves, which could be you, your neighbors, coworkers, or anyone else in your community. They offer all the usual banking services like savings accounts, loans, and checking accounts, but with a more personal touch.

One cool thing about credit unions is that they're not-for-profit organizations. So, instead of trying to make a bunch of money for shareholders, they focus on giving back to their members through lower fees, better interest rates, and sometimes even community programs. Plus, because they're smaller and more community-oriented, credit unions often provide really personalized customer service.

While credit unions have some awesome perks, there are a few drawbacks to consider too.

Credit unions usually have fewer physical branches than big banks. So, if you're someone who likes to do most of your banking in person or needs access to a lot of ATMs, you might find them inconvenient. Their online banking and mobile apps might not be as fancy or up-to-date either.

Another drawback is that credit unions might have slightly stricter membership requirements. While many are open to anyone who lives, works, or worships in a certain area, some have more specific criteria you need to meet to join. And because they're smaller, credit unions might not offer as wide of a range of financial products and services as big banks. It's important to weigh the pros and cons and see what works best for you!

Perfectly Calculated Direct Deposit

Direct deposit is the magic sauce in this systematic recipe. People use direct deposit in various ways, but the best way to use direct deposit is to your advantage.

Your direct deposit totals' accuracy strictly depends on how well you use your Flexible Budget™. Most employers will let you add up to five different accounts for direct deposit (but verify this first). You can choose either a percentage or an exact amount to be directed into your bank accounts. For this budgeting framework, you'll use the exact amount option.

Direct an exact amount of money into each of your three main bank accounts (this is why the first step was to obtain three different bank accounts at three different institutions). Having the exact amount of expenses, savings, and spending go directly into assigned accounts streamlines and automates payday. FinTech was created for your benefit, so use it.

What to do if your employer only allows one account for direct deposit!

If your employer is stuck in the Stone Ages and only allows ONE account to be attached for direct deposit (I'm sorry), you should still have three bank accounts, but one will serve as a "landing" account.

Your landing account should be your bill pay account. You will have to set up automatic transfers from your landing/bill pay account to your other two accounts.

Be mindful that it could take between 2–4 business days for the money to transfer between banking institutions. So, be diligent about how you spend on payday. You never want to overdraft your account before your funds have a chance to settle.

Automatic Bill Pay

Have you ever looked at your bank account and felt like there was (suspiciously) too much money in it? Then, later got an email saying you missed a payment, so you have a late fee on top of the original bill you forgot? Yeah, we've all been there.

Once you establish an exclusive bill pay account, all of your bills will be debited from the same place. And once all of your bills are debited from the same account, you can set up automatic payments. You will never miss a bill payment again. You should feel relieved already just thinking about all of your bills being paid on time.

The goal is to trick yourself into spending less and saving more. It's an added bonus if the creditor has an incentive for auto-pay setup. For instance, my student loan interest rate was reduced when I set up auto pay. I encourage you to take it one step further and set up automatic savings transfers as well.

Rich Tip:

Create small monthly payments in your budget for any bill that is paid quarterly, semi-annually, or annually. This way those bills dont sneak up on you when its time to pay.

Why Does This System Work?

This is the easiest way to follow the flow of your money because **money is a system!** Divide and conquer.

When our money is in one account, we tend to overspend or believe the illusion that we have more money than we actually do. Opening multiple accounts and giving each account a specific job is the most flexible way to spread your money while still having control of your funds.

Creating a system for your money will give you the relief you have been searching for. Instead of being an outsider, you'll be the CEO. This system gives you the ability to easily review what's working for your money and what isn't.

When you can quickly identify problem areas in the system, you can fix them, and the system can keep moving. Just like a car, your system will alert you when something is wrong, and knowing when something is wrong will give you the chance to fix the problem. I don't know about you, but I like my money simple and working for me.

Here's an example of what a money system will look like once it's set up. Take some time to review and get familiar with the system. Your system will start with your payday income. The arrows show where the money transfers within the system. You can take three actions with money on payday: spend it, save it, or invest it. If you're truly focused on building wealth, you need to do more saving and investing than spending.

Money System Example

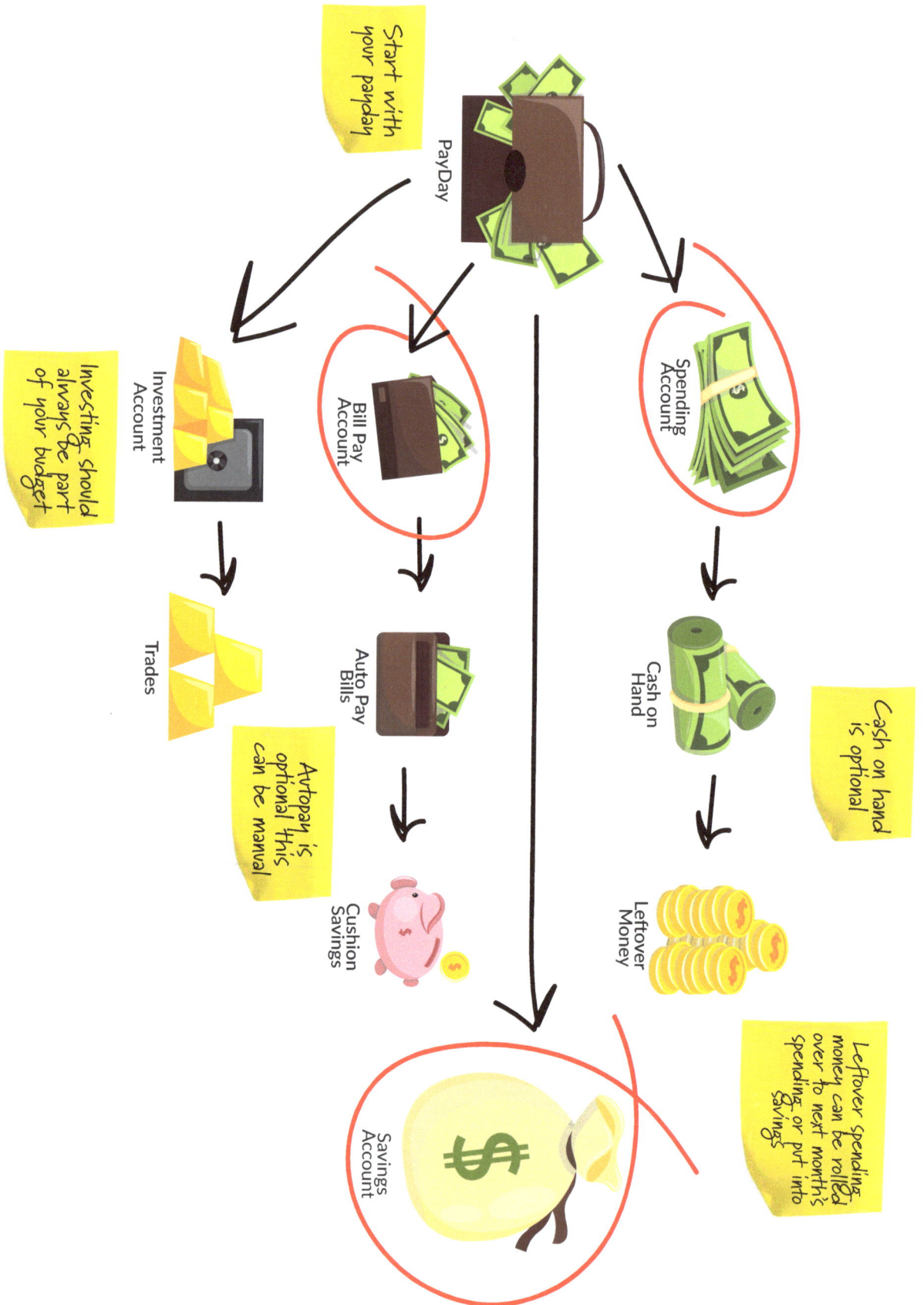

Start with your payday

PayDay

Investing should always be part of your budget

Investment Account

Trades

Bill Pay Account

Auto Pay Bills

Autopay is optional this can be manual

Cushion Savings

Spending Account

Cash on Hand

Cash on hand is optional

Leftover Money

Savings Account

Leftover spending money can be rolled over to next month's spending or put into savings

50

EXERCISE #10:
Build Your Money System

Instructions:

Draw your money system in the box below starting with your payday and including your three main bank accounts: bill pay, spending, and high-yield savings.

Section Key Points

- Become the CEO of your dollars. Money is a system. Start understanding how your money is moving.

- Separate your money into three different bank accounts and determine your New Zero.

- The banks need you. You are the customer; break up with any bank who forgets that.

- Turn on your bank notifications. There should never be any surprises with your money.

Reflect on your past broke feelings. What will your New Zero be so you don't feel broke again?

Which high yield savings account will you choose for your money system? Research 3 different banks and list their pros and cons.

Section Notes

YOUR INCOME IS IMPORTANT

SECTION OBJECTIVES

1. Identify the various sources of income you receive, and gain understanding of your financial inflows.

2. Learn step one in the Flexible Budget™ framework to equip yourself with the skills to assess the accuracy and consistency of your income.

3. Discover tools and techniques to create a comprehensive record-keeping system for your income.

WHY SHOULD YOU CARE?

Accuracy in Budgeting: Creating a realistic budget that aligns with your actual earnings helps you avoid overestimating or underestimating your income.

Identify Income Patterns: By analyzing your income records, you can identify seasonal fluctuations, trends, and unexpected windfalls. This information helps you understand your cash flow patterns and make proactive adjustments to your money system.

Clarity and Opportunities: Getting a clear overview of your earnings will help you make informed decisions about your budget, expenses, and financial goals. It'll also help you identify any discrepancies, inconsistencies, or missed opportunities for income growth.

Recording Income

Quick recap, by now you have:

1. Reviewed your past spending habits
2. Forgiven yourself for past spending habits
3. Created an airtight automatic money system

At this point, you're ahead of the game! Now it's time for the easiest part: creating the Flexible Budget™. The first step is identifying all of your income. (If you are an hourly or gig worker, skip this step and start with step two. It will be easier to determine how much money your income goal should be after calculating expenses, savings, and spending.)

Income is any money that you add to your pockets from an outside source. Salaries, side hustles, and investments, oh my! Multiple streams of income are a necessity nowadays; we can't rely on just one, but if you do only have a salary right now, it's fine!

Don't stress—side hustles will come later. You should always be thinking about ways to increase your income and add an extra stream wherever you can.

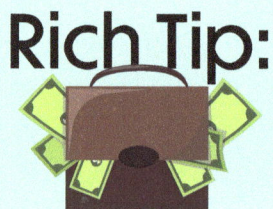

Rich Tip: Create your Flexible Budget™ to match your monthly payment schedule, whether you get paid weekly, biweekly, two times a month, or monthly.

Creating a bi-weekly Flexible Budget™ certainly changed the game for me. So, when you're filling out your information, be sure to divide your monthly income in half. This will give your ego an extra boost when reviewing monthly bill payments as well.

Find the digital copy of the Flexible Budget™ template here:
https://www.moneyinyour20s.com

Increasing Your Income

Here's the thing: you probably don't make enough money. I'm not calling you broke; this is just the dark reality for most people. It's true that many people have a money organization problem. However, some people have both an income problem and a money organization problem—a double whammy. There needs to be a point in your life when you give yourself a reality check about your income. Trying to budget when you don't have adequate income is like putting a band-aid on a broken arm.

The first place you need to look to increase your income is your current job. Is there a promotion you can apply to? When was the last time you requested a raise from your employer? It's more expensive for a company to hire someone new than to promote within. Gather all the evidence of how you have either cut costs or increased sales for the company. That's the secret sauce to encouraging a manager to agree to a salary increase. It's tempting to say, "Inflation is killing my check, and these bills ain't gonna pay themselves." But managers don't care about your financial issues; they care about how your work impacts their bottom line. There are three types of employees: those who SAVE the company money, those who EARN the company money, and those who COST the company money. Here's an insider tip: never be the employee costing the company money.

If your current company won't increase your pay, the next step is to decide whether to apply for positions at different companies or start a new side hustle. Doing both at the same time can cause you to become overwhelmed, so it may be best to just do one or the other.

There's a lot of energy required for both options. Applying and interviewing for new roles can be just as taxing as showing up to the office every day. It's absolutely possible for you to do both at the same time, but that's a decision for you and your brain to make. Remember, burnout is real, and it can take months to return to your regular self after a burn-down episode. Whichever option you choose, commit to it and see it through. You already have the framework for setting goals and creating action plans, but if you need a refresher, go back to the goal-setting section.

The next page has a decision tree to help you evaluate if starting a side hustle is right for you. When reflecting on skills and talents that can be turned into money, consider taking some of the tried-and-true personality quizzes available. This might sound silly, but quizzes such as Myers-Briggs, Clifton Strength Finder, Big Five Personality Test, and the DISC Assessment can help uncover your natural abilities. When you're in tune with your natural abilities, you'll be able to select careers and side hustles that come easy to you. This eliminates friction and gets you to that easy money quickly.

Decision Tree: Do You Need To Start A Side Hustle?

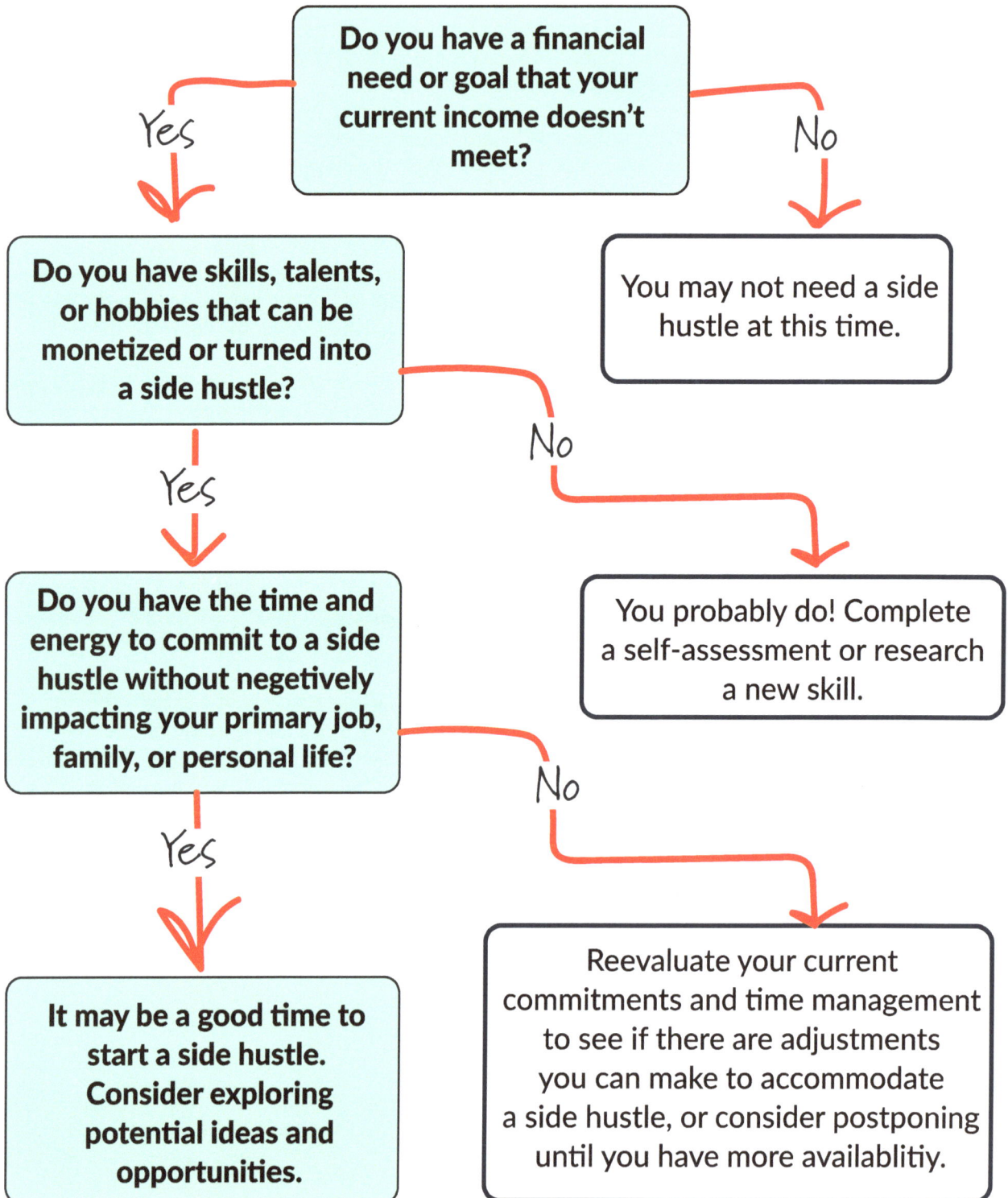

Do you have a financial need or goal that your current income doesn't meet?

Yes

No

Do you have skills, talents, or hobbies that can be monetized or turned into a side hustle?

You may not need a side hustle at this time.

No

Yes

Do you have the time and energy to commit to a side hustle without negetively impacting your primary job, family, or personal life?

You probably do! Complete a self-assessment or research a new skill.

No

Yes

It may be a good time to start a side hustle. Consider exploring potential ideas and opportunities.

Reevaluate your current commitments and time management to see if there are adjustments you can make to accommodate a side hustle, or consider postponing until you have more availablitiy.

Side Hustles

In the spirit of encouraging you to try something new, I'll share some side hustles I've done over the years to bring some extra dollars in. I gave them all my own personal "Yelp Review" and rated them out of 5 stars. On the next page, there is an additional list of side hustle ideas that can help supplement your main income.

Wedding Dress Consultant ⭐⭐⭐

Technically, I was employed. But as a wedding dress consultant at a chain wedding dress boutique, my shifts were only four hours a piece, and I was mostly paid via commission. So, I'm going to count this as a side hustle.

Food Delivery Driver ⭐

This was by far my least favorite side hustle. The deliveries were always stressful: parking, low tips, rude customers, and unbearable employees. I made decent money, but I would never do it again.

Online Tutor ⭐⭐⭐⭐

When you understand a unique subject matter, it's easy to stay booked. Fortunately for me, I'm good at accounting and got paid extra as an accounting tutor. Math and English are also in high demand at all times. You may have to take a knowledge test, but this is a very low-energy, high-reward side hustle.

Grocery Delivery ⭐⭐⭐

This was one of my absolute favorite side hustles, mainly because I genuinely love going grocery shopping. Unlike food delivery, there is always parking, the customer base is typically much nicer, and the tips are better. However, I didn't love all the miles it put on my car or the gas expenses.

16 EXTRA SIDE HUSTLE IDEAS

Become a secret shopper

Become a home inspector

Become an audio book reader

Participate in scientific studies

Be an extra for TV and movies

Online customer service

Become a notary public

Become a proofreader

Virtual Assistant

Become a house sitter

Dog walker/pet sitter

Join marketing focus groups

Create user generated content

Become a party entertainer

Sell stock photography

Flip thrift store finds

Flexible Budget™ Step One Example

If you get paid bi-weekly review both

Income Type	Monthly Earning	Bi-Weekly Earning
Salary	3,412.74	1,706.37
Side Hustle (tutoring)	250	125
Side Hustle (instacart)	250	50

Sometimes you need two side hustles!

Calcuate your total monthly income

Total Monthly Income $ 3,912.74

EXERCISE #11:
Flexible Budget™
Step One (Record Your Income)

Instructions:

In the table below, list all your monthly income and the total monthly earnings from each income type. Then, calculate your bi-weekly earnings by dividing your monthly earnings by two. Lastly, calculate your total monthly earnings and write in your sum.

Income Type	Monthly Earning	Bi-Weekly Earning

Total Monthly Income $ ⬚⬚⬚,⬚⬚⬚.⬚⬚

Step One: Recording Income

Section Key Points

- You probably aren't making enough money to live the life you really want to live.

- A side hustle is not always the best way to increase your income, do research and make a strategic evaluation to decide if it's best for you.

- Try increasing your main salary at your current job first. It's cheaper for them to keep you than hire someone new.

- Break down your budget based on how often you get paid.

What is ONE action you will take to increase your income?

How much money will you need to make monthly to feel comfortable?

Section Notes

HOW TO PAY YOUR BILLS

MONEY ON MY MIND!

SECTION OBJECTIVES

1. Learn ways to reduce your monthly expenses while maintaining a high quality of life.

2. Step-by-step instructions on creating categories and subcategories to classify expenses for analysis.

3. Interpret your expense data and utilize the insights gained to optimize your budgeting and spending habits.

WHY SHOULD YOU CARE?

Identify Expense Patterns and Opportunities: Recognizing patterns and trends in your expenses allows you to evaluate whether your spending aligns with your priorities.

Reducing Financial Waste: Assessing whether certain expenses align with your priorities and your dream life will help you make more conscious spending decisions and redirect your money toward what truly matters to you.

Clear Expense Insight: Reviewing and documenting your expenses empowers you to make informed financial decisions. With a thorough understanding of your expenses, you can evaluate the trade-offs associated with various choices.

Recording Recurring Bills

Step Two is all about identifying all your recurring bills. **Recurring bills are those predictable expenses that you pay monthly, quarterly, semi-annually, or annually.**

These are the bills you know are coming. These bills include living expenses such as a mortgage or rent and any memberships, subscriptions, or extra luxuries you spend money on to survive, thrive, and have fun. Be sure to include loan payments such as a car note, student loan, and any other debt payments as well.

Have you ever been confused because you know you have enough money to cover bills, but you still feel stretched thin between paydays? This problem is caused by too many bills withdrawing too close together.

Month:	November					
Sunday	Monday	Tuesday	Wednesday	Thursday	Friday	Saturday
	1 $	2 $	3	4	5 *Pay Day*	6
7	8	9	10 $	11	12 $	13
14	15	16	17	18 $	19 *Pay Day*	20
21	22	23 $	24	25	26 $	27
28 $	29	30				

Review all of your billing due dates. **If you find many of your bills are due around the same time, change it right now!** This is the perfect time to call or email those companies and negotiate a new due date. You want your due dates to fall in between paydays. For friends with monthly paydays, it might help to have a "bill day": one day of the month when all your bills are withdrawn from your account. When there are too many bills due at the beginning or end of the month, it can overwhelm your bank account. Sometimes, it's more about WHEN you pay your bills than about how much the bills are.

The last line item in Step Two is the cushion amount. Do not try to go without the cushion. This will help you in the long run for those bills that vary in cost. I'm talking about utilities like water, gas, and electricity.

You can never know the exact amount those bills will be, so having a cushion will help you during those months when your usage is higher than usual. An extra 5%–10% of your total monthly expenses is perfect for a cushion. This is where the bill pay savings account will come into play.

Be sure to set up an automatic transfer to move your cushion money into your bill pay savings account. Over time, this money will serve as extra sneaky savings baked into your system. You and your bank account will thank me later!

Negotiating Monthly Bills

Before we move on, we need to discuss the lost art of haggling. Haggling is a part of many cultures. Americans prefer to call it negotiating, but you can call it whatever you like. At the end of the day, it's sweet-talking your way into paying less for something you want or need.

Most service providers will negotiate your monthly bill payment amount.

Seriously! You just have to have the confidence and patience to call and negotiate your bills. Oftentimes, you're paying for random hidden fees and add-ons that you don't even use.

Here are some discounts you should ask about:

- Military
- Student
- Low Income
- Disablity

Calling your service provider may make you nervous, but remember, you have nothing to lose, and so, so much to gain. You'll be talking to a customer service representative whose main objective is to keep you a customer. When in doubt, threaten to cancel your entire account and watch them scramble. Remember to remain patient, calm, and kind when chatting with the customer service representative. **AND TAKE NOTES!**

These are the most commonly negotiated bills:

- Cell Phone
- Wi-Fi
- Cable
- Credit Card including limit, fees, and interest rate
- Healthcare
- Gym membership

This workbook includes a sample script for calling service providers and a worksheet to help you keep track of the ones you contact.

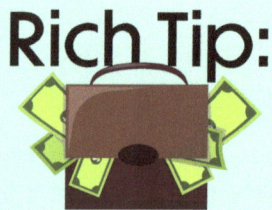

Rich Tip:

When in doubt, ask to speak to the supervisor or manager. Most times they we be more helpful when getting fees removed or lowered.

Now that you've calculated your income and expenses, it's time to discuss discretionary funds and disposable income.

The terms "Disposable Income" and "Discretionary Funds" are always thrown around, so let me explain the difference.

Disposable income is defined as income remaining after tax deductions and other mandatory charges, available to be spent or saved as one wishes. This is Oxford's definition, not mine.

Discretionary funds are defined as funds remaining after tax deductions, other mandatory charges, and expenditures on necessary items. Again, this is Oxford's definition, not mine.

That's right: they're the same exact thing.

The short version is income minus mandatory expenses. Whatever money you have left over is the amount you have available to invest, save or spend on whatever you want.

It's important to know how much disposable income you have because when it's time to make new money moves, invest in a new opportunity, or aggressively pay down debt, you'll need to know how much money you have available to use.

The beauty of the Flexible Budget™ is that once your bills are paid, you have the freedom to invest, save and spend at your leisure. Gone are the days when you have to predict how much money you'll spend on random items throughout the month.

Does it truly matter if your bills are paid and your savings are stacked?

EXERCISE #12:
Planning Your Monthly Expenses

Instructions:

On the "Current Monthly Bill Cycle" calendar below, mark all of your paydays. Then, mark all the days your recurring monthly bills are due. On the "Ideal Monthly Bill Cycle," mark your current paydays. Then, organize ideal dates for your new bill pay cycle.

Current Monthly Bill Cycle

Sunday	Monday	Tuesday	Wednesday	Thursday	Friday	Saturday
	1	2	3	4	5	6
7	8	9	10	11	12	13
14	15	16	17	18	19	20
21	22	23	24	25	26	27
28	29	30	31			

Ideal Monthly Bill Cycle

Sunday	Monday	Tuesday	Wednesday	Thursday	Friday	Saturday
	1	2	3	4	5	6
7	8	9	10	11	12	13
14	15	16	17	18	19	20
21	22	23	24	25	26	27
28	29	30	31			

Script to Negotiate Your Bills

You: Hi (Service Provider), I reviewed last month's bill, and I would like to understand the breakdown of my bill.

Rep: Of course, (gives you the rundown).

You: Ok, thank you is there a way I can lower my monthly bill to $xxxx a month?

Rep: There is another package you may qualify for that is closer to that price how does that sound?

You: What other discounts do I qualify for to get closer to my desired price? I would like to keep this service, but if I cannot get my bill down to $xx.xx price I will have to cancel the service or switch to a competitor with lower costs.

Rep: Ah, let me check with my manager to see what we can do for you.

You: Thank you so much for understanding!

Rep: My manager has approved this change have a great day!

*If the representative gives you a hard time, ask to speak to the manager. I know that sounds whiny, but that may be the key to saving $10–$15 a month for the exact same service you're already receiving.

EXERCISE #13:
Negotiating Your Current Bills

Instructions:

Call your current service providers and use the bill negotiation script to request changes and reductions. The first example is done for you.

DATE	TIME	SERVICE PROVIDER	REP NAME	CURRENT PAYMENT	WHAT ARE YOU PAYING FOR?	NEW PRICE	COMMENTS
3/28	11:42 am	pyc co.	Jamie	$69.99	20 gigs of data, router rental	$19.99	reduced to 10 gigs

Flexible Budget™ Step Two Example

Category	Monthly Expenses	Bi-Weekly Expenses
Rent	850	425
Hulu	11.99	6.00
Tidal Music	9.99	5.00
Phone	50	25
Car Insurance	183.33	91.67
Student Loans	100	50
Car Note	300	150
Credit Card	37	18.50
Gym	10	5
Utilities	45	22.50
Buffer	50	25

I pay car insurance twice a year, but I set aside monthly payments towards my bill

This is the minimum balance

Estimated total

Include a buffer to your budget

Add your total expenses

Total Monthly Expense $ 1,647.31

Act Rich, Be Responsible

EXERCISE #14:
Flexible Budget™
Step Two [Record Your Expenses]

Instructions:

In the table below, list all your monthly expenses and the total monthly cost for each. Then, calculate your bi-weekly expenses by dividing your monthly costs by two. Lastly, calculate your total monthly expenses and write in your sum.

Expense Type	Monthly Costs	Bi-Weekly Costs

Total Monthly Expense $ ___,___.__

Disposable Income Example

Total income was calculated in Step One

Total Monthly Income $ 3,912.74

SUBTRACT

If your INCOME is less than your expenses there is a problem!

Total expenses were calculated in Step Two

Total Monthly Expense $ 1,647.31

EQUALS

Total money leftover after bills are paid

Disposable Income $ 2,265.43

Goal: Make enough money from my side hustle to cover monthly expenses

Act Rich, Be Responsible

EXERCISE #15:
Calculate Disposable Income

Instructions:

Write in your total monthly income calculated in Step One. Write in your total monthly expenses calculated in Step Two. Calculate disposable income by subtracting income from expenses.

Total Monthly Income

$ 000,000.00

SUBTRACT

If your INCOME is less than your expenses there is a problem!

Total Monthly Expense

$ 000,000.00

EQUALS

Disposable Income

$ 000,000.00

Step Two: Recording Recurring Bills

Section Key Points

- Sometimes, WHEN you pay your bills have a huge impact on your budget and organization.

- Bills are negotiable. It never hurts to ask your service provider for a price reduction or to change the due date.

- Start saving for quarterly, semi-annually, and annually paid expenses so they won't catch you by surprise.

- If your INCOME is less than your EXPENSES, there is a problem!

Reflect on your current expenses. Do your expenses align with the goals you have set for your money?

How do you plan on redirecting your expenses to align with your current goals? What should be eliminated? What should be reduced?

Section Notes

PAYING YOUR FUTURE SELF

SECTION OBJECTIVES

1. Create a system to review, assess, and automate your savings goals on a regular basis.

2. Be equipped with practical techniques to enhance clarity, organization and progress tracking.

3. Learn how to identify potential obstacles to maximize the chances of savings success.

WHY SHOULD YOU CARE?

Accountability and Motivation: Regularly reviewing your savings allows you to assess your progress, identify any gaps or challenges, and adjust your strategies accordingly. This provides a sense of achievement as you see your savings grow.

Transparency Enhances Focus: Documenting your savings helps you visualize your aspirations, making them more attainable.

Prioritize Savings: Saving is about paying your future self for the life you deserve to live. Making your savings a priority gets you closer to your dream life.

Automate Savings Goals

If you've made it to this step, that means you know exactly how much money you have left over after your bills are paid. Now that you know this, it's time to save your money!

You MUST establish a save first, spend last mindset. When you save before you spend, you truly win. Many people preach the pay yourself first idea, but if your bills aren't paid first, you won't survive to pay yourself.

There are two types of savings: permanent and temporary. Temporary savings are also known as sinking funds. A sinking fund is money you have saved with the intent to spend. Most money you save will be in a sinking fund.

Examples of sinking funds are fun funds, new house funds, and debt payment funds. Sinking funds are how you finance your future best life. Create your savings goals using the sticky goals exercise on page 24.

Permanent savings, on the other hand, are meant to stay in your bank account and grow WITHOUT withdrawals.

An example of long-term savings is an emergency fund.

Emergency funds are important because the unexpected will always happen. I've found that the best way to hit savings goals is to start small and build up. Having $10,000 in your emergency fund may seem out of your reach if you have $0.00 saved right now. But $10,000 is just 100 hundred-dollar bills in one place.

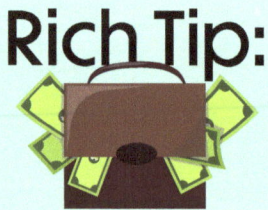

Rich Tip:

Treat your savings like your bills and make them mandatory. Make your future self a priority.

Emergency Fund vs Sinking Fund

Your emergency fund and your sinking fund are not built the same. Emergency funds are there to keep you afloat if you lose your primary source of income or if something unexpected happens. It's your safety net to ensure you won't go into debt or be in financial distress when the uncontrollable happens. Typically, you don't plan to spend your emergency fund money.

Sinking funds are dollars you save with the sole intention of spending, whether it's on a vacation, concert tickets, or a house. The money in your sinking fund will one day be gone in exchange for the life you imagined for the future.

When establishing your sinking fund, there are two methods of execution: having one big sinking pot for all your fun (or whenever you wanna live it all the way up) or having different buckets (multiple accounts). Choose the method you want depending on what makes sense in your brain. Don't worry. If you test one method out and it doesn't tickle your fancy, you can always change it. If you feel uncomfortable at any point in time, you have the power to reset and adjust

Rich Tip:

Your savings rate can increase when you figure out how to grow your DISPOSABLE INCOME. That means increasing your income and maintaining or lowering your monthly expenses.

Establishing Your Emergency Fund

Emergency funds are not only needed in cases of job loss—shocking, I know! While we often see emergency funds tied to job loss, that is not their only purpose. They can also supplement income from hospitalization, home repairs, or car issues. The best emergency funds are the ones that can take a hit.

Strive to save between 3–6 months of survive and thrive expenses in your emergency fund (refer to page 35). Try implementing a save-first strategy. I suggest you have an aggressive savings strategy before committing to an aggressive debt payment strategy.

It makes *NO SENSE* to aggressively pay off debt only to end up with zero dollars in savings. The best thing about saving aggressively first is that you will feel less stress when paying off debt. This approach gives you the flexibility to pivot your funds after you hit your savings goals.

Here's how you determine your perfect savings number:

Housing Mortgage, Rent, and Property Tax	$850
Utilities Electricity, Water, Cell Phone, and Gas	$95
Groceries This does not include eating out	$200
Transportation Basic average gas, or public transportation	$343
Minimum Debt Credit Cards, Auto Loans, and Student Loans	$437
Min. Cost of Living	**$1,925**

Emergency Fund Goal Example

01

Category	Monthly Spending	Bi-Weekly Spending
Rent	850	425
Phone	50	25
Car Insurance	183.33	91.67
Student Loans	100	50
Car Note	300	150
Credit Card	37	18.50
Utilities	45	22.50
Groceries	200	100

Review expenses from Step 2 and remove anything that is not a Survive or Thrive expense.

Estimate a grocery budget.

02 Sum up your total survive and thrive expenses.

$$\$1765.33$$

Minimum Cost of Living

This total will be less than the total calculated in Step 2.

03 How many months of minimum expenses do you want to save?

6
Months

This could be 3, 6, 12, or 18 months depending on your lifestyle and spending habits.

$$\$1765.33 \quad \times \quad 6 \quad =$$

Minimum Cost of Living   **Months**

This is the number you need to reach in order to have a fully funded savings account.

04 Total Emergency Fund Goal $ 1 0 , 5 9 1 . 9 8

83

Act Rich, Be Responsible

EXERCISE #16:
Emergency Fund Goal

Instructions:

In the exercise below, list all of your survive and thrive expenses found in Step Two. Calculate one month's worth of Survive and Thrive expenses. Multiply your monthly expenses by the number of months you would like to save for to determine your emergency fund savings goal.

01

Category	Monthly Spending	Bi-Weekly Spending

02 Sum up your total survive and thrive expenses. _____

Minimum Cost of Living

03 How many months of minimum expenses do you want to save? _____

Months

_____ **X** _____ **=**

Minimum Cost of Living   **Months**

04 Total Emergency Fund Goal $ ☐☐☐ , ☐☐☐ . ☐☐

Starting Slow

The last thing to remember about saving money is that it's a privilege. Give yourself grace and space to build your savings over time. Starting with $5 a day is more than enough to build the habit of paying future you. Soon, that $5 will grow into $50 and eventually $500. Every little step you take compounds on itself. A year from now, you'll be in a completely different financial situation. If it's moving too slowly for your taste, start that side hustle, apply for that new job, or demand that promotion. Focus on increasing your disposable income as much as possible. You will use those funds to create the future you know you deserve. If you believe future you deserves pickle juice, continue to drink pickle juice. If you believe future you deserves the finest wines and fancy ginger shots, give them the money to buy it.

Decision Tree: Should You Use Your Emergency Fund?

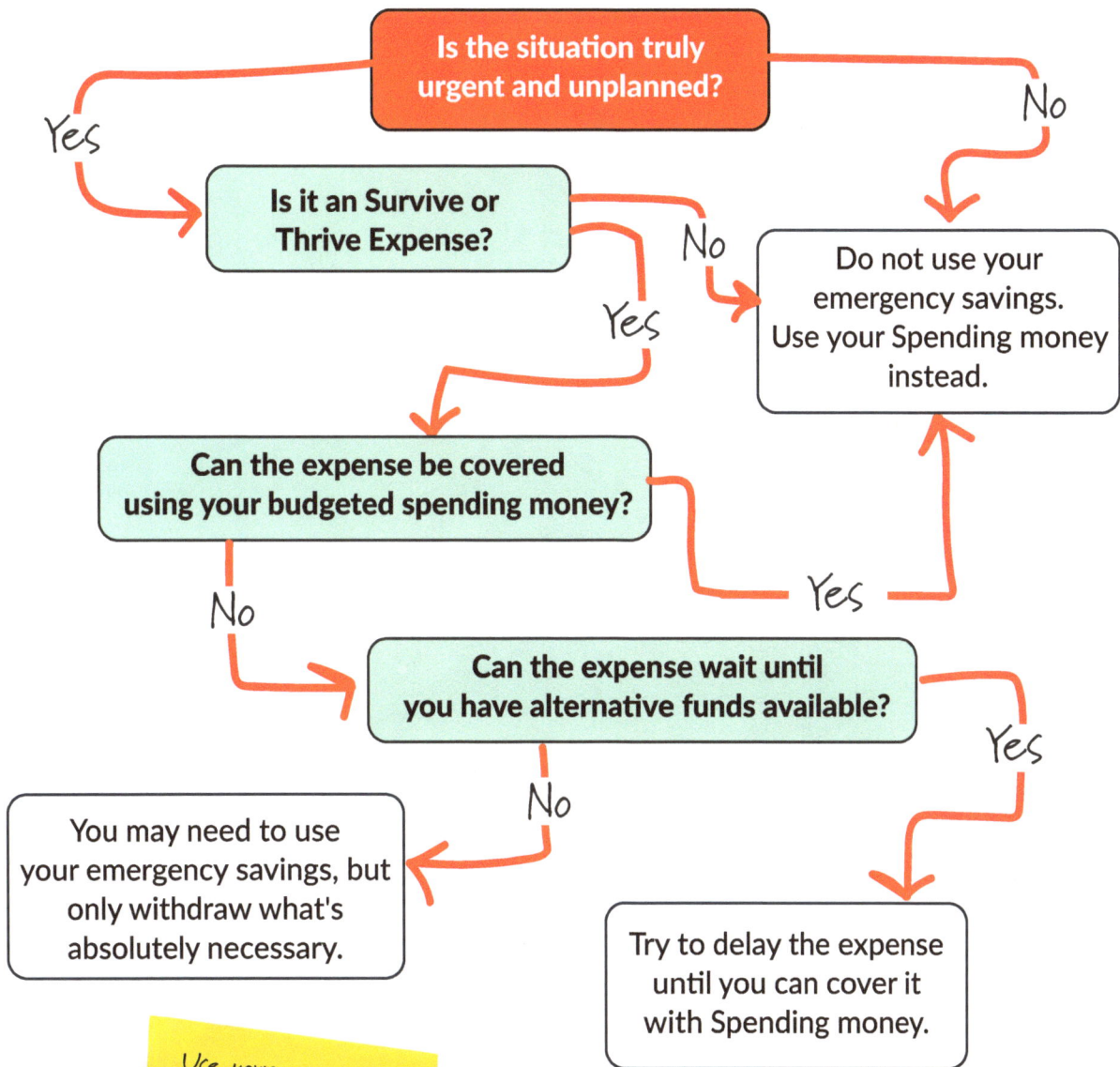

Is the situation truly urgent and unplanned?

Yes → **Is it an Survive or Thrive Expense?**

No → Do not use your emergency savings. Use your Spending money instead.

Is it an Survive or Thrive Expense?

No → Do not use your emergency savings. Use your Spending money instead.

Yes → **Can the expense be covered using your budgeted spending money?**

Can the expense be covered using your budgeted spending money?

Yes → Do not use your emergency savings. Use your Spending money instead.

No → **Can the expense wait until you have alternative funds available?**

Can the expense wait until you have alternative funds available?

Yes → Try to delay the expense until you can cover it with Spending money.

No → You may need to use your emergency savings, but only withdraw what's absolutely necessary.

Use your emergency savings, but create a plan to replenish it as soon as possible.

Try to explore other options (e.g., borrowing from family, friends, or a low-interest loan) before tapping into your emergency savings.

Flexible Budget™ Step Three Example

Savings Goals	Monthly Savings	Bi-Weekly Savings
Emergency Fund	700	350
Roth IRA/ Retirement	100	50
Fun Fund	300	125
Debt Payment	300	150

Aggressive Savings first

NOT a 401 (k) account.

Future best life fund!

Put money aside to pay off debt.

This is in addition to the minimum payment

The goal is to have more savings than expenses

Total Monthly Savings $ 1,400.00

EXERCISE #17:
Flexible Budget™ Step Three [Set Savings Goals]

Instructions:

In the exercise below write in your total disposable income calculated in Step 2. Write in your total monthly savings calculated in Step 3. Calculate disposable income by subtracting disposable income from total savings.

Savings Goals	Monthly Savings	Bi-Weekly Savings

Total Monthly Savings

$ 000,000.00

Money Available to Spend Example

Disposable Income $ 2,265.43

Income minus expenses.

SUBTRACT

Total Monthly Savings $ 1,400.00

Calcuated in Step Three

EQUALS

Spending Allowance $ 1,865.43

This flows from your income out to your spending.

Act Rich, Be Responsible

Calculate Money Available to Spend

Instructions:

In the exercise below write in your total disposable income calculated in Step 2. Write in your total monthly savings calculated in Step 3. Calculate disposable income by subtracting disposable income from total savings.

Disposable Income $ 000,000.00

SUBTRACT

Total Monthly Savings $ 000,000.00

EQUALS

Spending Allowance $ 000,000.00

Act Rich, Be Responsible

EXERCISE #19:
Savings Tracker

Instructions:

Use the exercise below during your savings journey to remain motivated and monitor your progress. As your savings grow, shade in your progress.

Savings Goal: $

| 100% |
| 95% |
| 90% |
| 85% |
| 80% |
| 75% |
| 70% |
| 65% |
| 60% |
| 55% |
| 50% |
| 45% |
| 40% |
| 35% |
| 30% |
| 25% |
| 20% |
| 15% |
| 10% |
| 5% |
| 0% |

Start Date

End Date

What am I saving for?

Why is this savings important?

Section Key Points

- Automating your savings will put you in the right place to hit your savings goals without any heavy lifting.

- Your emergency savings should be 3–6 months of your survive and thrive expenses. (See S.T.I.F.F Formula™ on page 33)

- Emergency savings and sinking funds are NOT the same things. They are different and should be treated as such.

- Saving is a marathon, not a sprint. Take your time to build; it's more than okay to start with $5 a day.

After reviewing your goals and your disposable income, do you believe you have enough money to reach your savings goals in your set timeframe?

Describe what it will feel like to hit your savings goal.

Section Notes

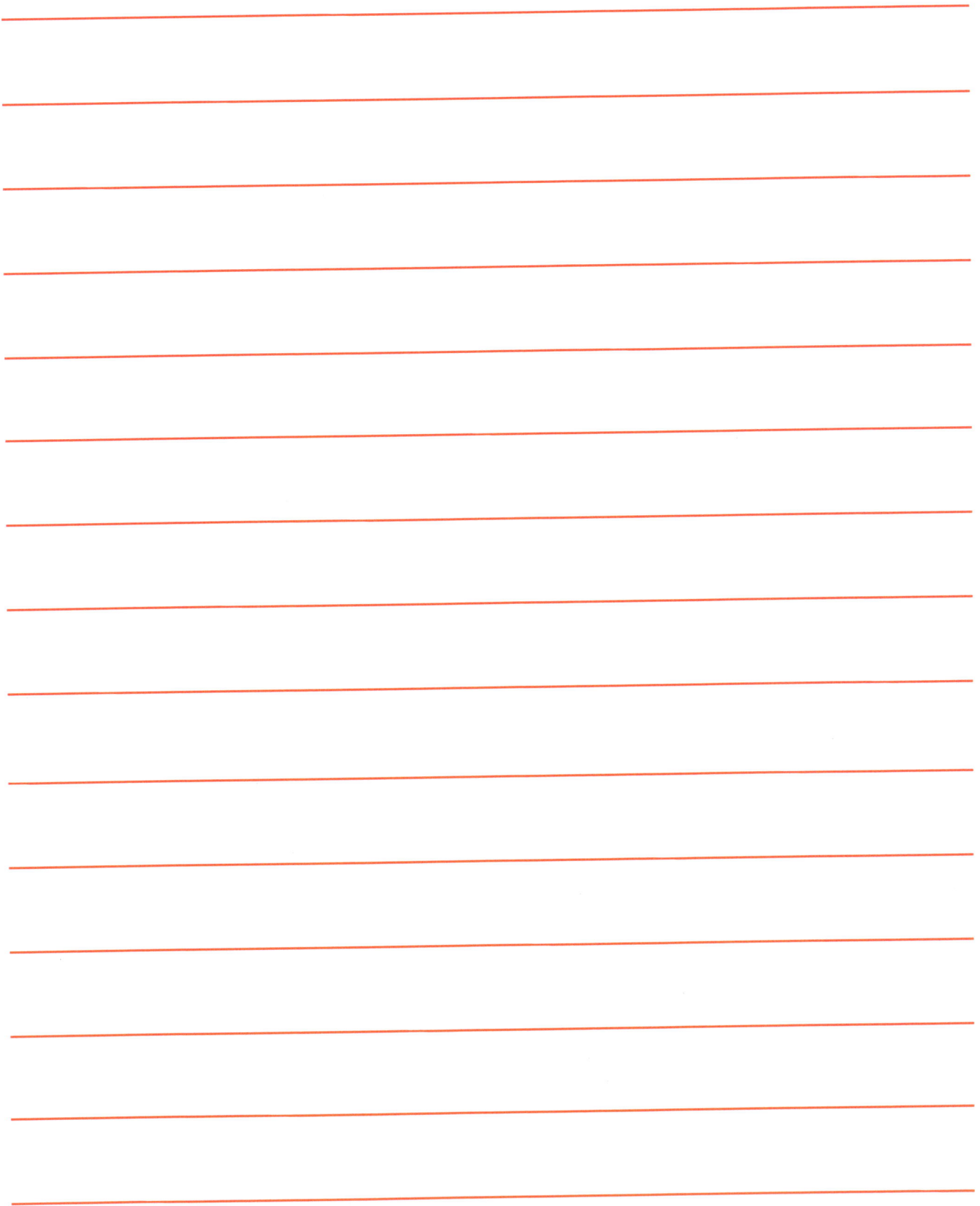

BUY NOW, OR PAY LATER?

SECTION OBJECTIVES

1. Discuss the process of evaluating current spending habits and identifying areas where adjustments can be made.

2. Provide guidance on avoiding impulsive or unnecessary purchases and making informed decisions to ensure spending allowance is not exceeded.

3. Learn about the fundamental aspects of using credit cards and Buy Now, Pay Later apps as alternative spending methods.

WHY SHOULD YOU CARE?

Reduce Financial Stress and Guilt: You can spend money guilt-free, knowing that you're staying within your designated limits while still achieving your money goals.

Practice Mindful Spending: Regularly reviewing your spending allowance can help you identify areas where you may be overspending or areas where you can make

Understand Your Spending Options: Today's technology makes it easy to spend your money. Learning how to manage credit cards and other payment options will help you develop more intentional spending practices.

Act Rich, Be Responsible

EXERCISE #20:
Spender Quiz

Instructions:

Answer each question below to find out what type of spender you are!

What Kind of Spender Are You?

---

1) Do you make a list before you grocery shopping?
A. What list? (No)
B. Yes, and I NEVER buy extra items
C. Yes, but sometimes I buy extra items

2) How do you feel about store-brand food?
A. Absolutely not! Name brand or nothing!
B. It's the only option; why would I waste money on overpriced brand-name food?!
C. There's nothing wrong with it, but some name brands taste better.

3) What do you consider a "major purchase"?
A. Any purchase totaling more than 3 months' salary.
B. Any purchase over $100.
C. Any purchase totaling more than 1 month's salary.

4) How do you plan for a major purchase?
A. Put it on the credit card and figure it out later
B. Wait for it to go on sale (no matter how long it takes)
C. Create a sinking fund and plan to purchase in 1-3 months.

5) Has social media ever influenced you to buy anything?
A. Ugh, too many times to count
B. No, never
C. Yes, but it takes some convincing

6) **Your friends invite you out for the night, but you don't get paid until next week. How do you respond?**

A. Agree to the dinner and use your credit card. It's okay; you get paid next week!

B. Leave them on read; they should know you don't like spending money unnecessarily.

C. Suggest a free/low-cost activity so you don't blow your budget.

7) **You found the PERFECT item to add to your closet, but it costs half your paycheck. What do you do?**

A. Buy it and figure it out later! Nothing is better than the original.

B. DIY it! No way I will be spending that type of money.

C. Find the dupe. It's just as cute for half the price.

8) **You and your friends are trying to get the vacation out of the group chat. Are you going?**

A. Only if the cheap people don't try to stick to a strict budget. I only vacation in style.

B. Only if we get the cheapest options possible; nothing is wrong with a budget-friendly airline and hotel.

C. Only if we can have a compromise. There are some things I can go cheap on, but others I refuse to.

9) **Your smartphone is completely broken; You need a new phone, what do you think is the best option?**

A. Buy the latest model. If you have to buy something new, it needs to be the best.

B. Ask your sister for her old phone. It's from five years ago, but it's free, and it works.

C. Start comparing prices for models, find the best price, and adjust your budget for the new expense.

10) **Your favorite artist just announced their summer tour! You really want to go, how do you afford the tickets?**

A. Get the best seats in the house and figure it out later.

B. Get a job at the stadium they will be performing at to watch for free.

C. Use money from your Fun Fund to buy tickets within budget.

Scoring Rubric

Review your answer choices and total up your points to discover your spending personality.

A = Two Points
B = One Point
C = Zero Points

Total Score: _____

If your total score equals...

[14-20] You are a **Certified Overspender**
A Certified Overspender throws caution (and money) to the wind. Your spending habits are to buy now and think about it later. Oftentimes, you get a thrill from buying new things. Making your life easier by paying for convenience is how you handle adversity.

Favorite Certified Overspender Phrase:
"I'm gonna make that money right back!"

[6-13] You are a **Cheapskate Spender**
A Cheapskate Spender is only concerned with one thing...the price. You're the person who wants to get everything at a discount to keep costs to a minimum. Spending money is one of your least favorite things to do. If there's a way to save money, you'll find it.

Favorite Cheapsake Spender Phrase
"Is it on sale?"

[0-5] You are a **Intentional Spender**
An Intentional Spender knows their habits and their money very well. Your spending habits are carefully planned, with a little room for random fun. You usually stick to your budget, but even when you stumble, there's a way to troubleshoot to get back on track.

Favorite Intentional Spender Phrase
"Let me make sure I have space in my budget."

Improving Your Spending Habits

No matter what you scored, there's room for improvement. The goal is to become an intentional spender. This looks like sticking to your budget, planning out your major purchases, and creating strong boundaries around your spending.

If you are an Overspender...

Check Your B.A.N.K™ (more on page 138)

Before making a purchase, ask yourself if it aligns with your values and priorities. Consider whether the item or experience will truly enhance your life in a meaningful way. By being more conscious of your spending decisions, you can avoid impulse purchases and focus on what truly matters to you.

Practice Delayed Gratification

Implement a waiting period before making a purchase, especially for non-essential items. Give yourself at least 24 hours to consider whether you really need the item or if it's just a fleeting desire. Start a spending wish list to remind yourself of potentially exciting purchases.This can help curb impulse spending and ensure your purchases are intentional.

Create Spending Boundaries

These rules and boundaries are set by you for you! Establishing clear boundaries can provide direction for your spending. Whether it's how you pay, when you pay, or what you pay for, having specific rules in place can help prioritize your spending and make it easier to resist impulse buys that don't align with your objectives.

If you are a Cheapskate Spender...

Identify Values and Priorities

Define clear priorities and identify your values and long-term aspirations. By aligning spending with these values, you can ensure that each purchase serves a purpose and contributes to your overall well-being. Whether it's investing in personal development, supporting causes they believe in, or nurturing relationships.

Invest in Quality Over Quantity

Sometimes spending a little more upfront on a higher-quality item can save money in the long run. Prioritize purchases that offer good value for their money and are built to last, rather than always looking for the cheapest option. Whether it's clothing, appliances, or electronics, investing in quality can lead to greater satisfaction and longevity.

Embrace the Joy of Occasional Splurges

Set aside a small portion of your money for discretionary spending on things that bring you joy. By allowing for these indulgences in moderation, you can maintain their frugality while still enjoying life.

If you are an Intentional Spender...

Recognizing your spending habits and consciously choosing to become intentional is an achievement in itself. It demonstrates your awareness and determination to take control of your financial journey.

Each step you take toward intentional spending, no matter how small, is a cause for celebration, whether you're cutting back on unnecessary purchases, setting a boundary, or just saying no. Embrace the journey and focus on your priorities—allow them to guide your financial decisions. Remember that setbacks are opportunities for growth, and each challenge you overcome strengthens you.

By being intentional with your spending, you're not just managing your finances; you're building a pathway toward the life you desire. Stay inspired by the progress you've made and the goals you're working toward. Surround yourself with support and practice self-compassion along the way. Visualize the life you're striving for and believe in your ability to achieve it. You are worth the investment. Your commitment to intentional spending is a testament to your dedication to your future rich self.

Spending Allowance

The finish line is close! Step Four is all about spending because money is meant to be spent. I only support healthy spending habits, though. Since you've made it to Step Four, that means your bills are paid and your money is saved.

When spending, it's best to keep it simple. So, I have four line items: *gas/transportation, groceries, cash on hand, and spending.* This is strategically listed in order of importance.

Since the cost of gas and groceries can vary, it's best to pick a limit that makes the most sense for you. I drive to work, so I have a gas budget of $40 weekly, or $160 monthly. Most weeks, I spend less than $40 on gas, but I want to be sure to give my budget space for fluctuating gas prices.

For groceries, I have a budget of $70 a week, or $280 monthly. Every grocery trip is different, but I try to stay close to my $70 weekly limit. Sometimes, I go over that amount, and when that happens, I try to spend less on the next trip.

Give yourself space to make mistakes and correct them.

Cash on hand is for those small purchases. Personally, anything under $10 is paid with cash. If I don't have the cash, I don't buy. Every time I get paid, I take out $60 in cash. Once the cash is gone, it's gone.

The last line item is spending. Whatever you have left is what you spend. When setting up your direct deposit, list your spending account last. It will automatically deposit the leftover funds that weren't deposited into your bill pay or savings accounts.

Since you're only spending from one account now, it'll be easy to review and make adjustments. If you're anything like me, then things can look differently from month to month, so trying to predict how much you'll spend on every little thing can be exhausting. Remember, as long as you spend within your limit, it doesn't matter what you spend your money on.

Okay, so I said there were four main spending categories—don't kill me, but that was a lie. If you remember, at the beginning of the workbook, we allocated 10% of our earnings to investing. This is because making your money work for you is necessary for growing your wealth.

Lucky for you, thanks to the power of FinTech, you have a lot of different investment options. The number of apps and services available for investing makes it more accessible than ever before. **There NEEDS to be a line item in your spending dedicated to investing.**

Spending Allowance Breakdown Example

Category	Monthly Spending	Bi-Weekly Spending
Gas/transportation	100	50
Groceries	150	75
Cash on hand	40	20
Spending	184.16	92.08
Acorns (Investment)	391.27	195.64

Ubers count as transportation

Always have some cash

Spend on whatever you want

10% of the total income to investing

Spending Allowance $ [ ] [ ] [ ] , 8 6 5 . 4 3

Disposable income minus savings

EXERCISE #21:
Flexible Budget™ Step Four [Spending Allowance]

Instructions:

In the exercise below, write in your spending allowance that was calculated in Step Three (page 90). List your spending categories and the total monthly spending allowance for each goal. Then, calculate your bi-weekly spending by dividing your monthly spending by two.

Category	Monthly Spending	Bi-Weekly Spending

Spending Allowance $ ☐☐☐,☐☐☐.☐☐

Spending Boundaries

Boundaries aren't only for crazy family members and friends. You need to create boundaries for your money too. Saying "NO" can be hard, but creating a financial "no-no" list will help you outline the boundaries you need to set with yourself to keep you on the right track. The word "no" can feel negative, but think of it this way: saying no to one thing allows you to say yes to another. Setting these boundaries will help your finances have consistency and order. It will also serve as a way for you to acknowledge those bad money habits you've been holding on to. You didn't think you would go through this book without addressing those nasty habits, did you?

Here are the rules for your financial no-no list:
- For every no, there must be a yes!
- Limit your no-no list to three things
- Make it relevant

Once you create your list, STICK TO IT! Nobody likes a flake, so keep the promises you make, even to yourself.

Lastly, there is no time limit for this list. Your no-no list is basically new standards and boundaries you set for the rest of your life. This is not just a random "no spend" month. This is you creating the guidelines for your money system from this point forward. Be intentional and strategic.

Rules for Spending Example
#1 Eat out days are weekends only
#2 Use cash for purchases under $10
#3 Flights over 5 hours upgrade to comfort plus
#4 One luxury purchase over $200 every quarter
#5 No new makeup shopping until use current products

Act Rich, Be Responsible

EXERCISE #22:
Spending Rules

Instructions:

Set your spending boundaries and give yourself 2–3 rules to follow for the next month. Make sure these rules align with the current goals you set on page 24. Use the example above for inspiration.

Using Credit Cards in Your Money System

I know you're probably wondering, "How do credit cards fit into my money system?" Whether you already have a credit card or are considering getting your first one, credit cards can be a great addition to any money system when used wisely and correctly.

Credit cards allow users to borrow money from their financial institution up to a predetermined credit limit, with the requirement to repay the borrowed amount along with any accrued interest and fees. An easy way to remember the difference is the debit card decreases when used for purchases, and the credit card increases.

Credit cards have a bad reputation, but I want to change that. Using a credit card is like having an open-book test. When you learn where to find all your credit card information, it'll be easy to incorporate one into your money system. When you open a new credit account, you're provided with paperwork detailing your total credit limit, annual percentage rate (APR), monthly statement period, due date, credit card benefits, potential penalties, annual fees, and other important information.

Some benefits to using credit cards over debit cards:

1. Fraud Protection: You won't be held liable for unauthorized transactions if your card is stolen or used fraudulently. In addition, credit cards typically offer dispute resolution processes, allowing you to challenge charges for goods or services that were not as described or were never received.

2. Rewards and Perks: Many credit cards offer rewards programs that allow cardholders to earn cash back, points, or miles on their purchases. These rewards can add up over time and be redeemed for travel, merchandise. statement credits, or gift cards. Additionally, credit cards may come with perks such as travel insurance, purchase protection, extended warranties. and access to airport lounges.

3. Build Credit History: Responsible credit card use can help you build a positive credit history, which is important for future financial endeavors such as applying for loans or mortgages. You can improve your credit score over time by making on-time payments and keeping your credit utilization low.

Debit Card vs Credit Card Example

DEBIT CARD

1234 5678 9012 345

Debit Card Statement

Beginning Balance $500

Purchase 1	$24
Purchase 2	$95
Purchase 3	$13
Purchase 4	$88
Purchase 5	$121

Debit Card Statement

Total Purchases $341

Ending Balance $159

CREDIT CARD

□□□□ □□□□ □□□□ □□□□

Credit Card Statement

Beginning Balance $100

Purchase 1	$24
Purchase 2	$95
Purchase 3	$13
Purchase 4	$88
Purchase 5	$121

Total Purchases $341

Statement Balance $441
Minimum Payment $35

Reading Your Credit Card Statement

Your Bank Name

(A) **Bank Card**

Account number ending in 1234
Open Date: Oct 24, 2024 · Close Date: Nov 23, 2024
Cardmember since 2018

(B)

ACCOUNT SUMMARY

Previous Balance	$6,770.89
Payments and Credits	$5,836.00
Purchases	$7.82
Balance Transfers	$0.00
Cash Advances	$0.00
Fees Charged	$0.50
Interest Charged	$0.00
New Balance	$943.21

See Interest Charge Calculation Section following the Transaction section for detailed **APR** information

Credit Line	$8,900
Credit Line Available	$7,956
Cash Advance Credit Line	$1,100
Cash Advance Credit Line Available	$1,100

You may be able to avoid interest on Purchases. See reverse for details.

FICO **(H)**
766

Your FICO Credit Score on 11/17/24.
More on Yourbank.com

(C)

PAYMENT INFORMATION

New Balance	**$943.21** **(D)**
Minimum Payment Due	$35.00 **(E)**
Payment Due Date	December 18, 2014

(F) **Late Payment Warning:** If we do not recieve your minimum payment by the date listed above, you may have to pay a late fee of up to $35.00 and your purchase and balance transfer APRs for new transactions may be increased up to the Penalty APR of 24.99% variable.

Minimum Payment Warning: If you make only the minimum payment each period, you will pay more in interest and it will take you longer to pay off your balance. For example:

If you make no additional charges using this card and each month you pay...	You will pay off the balance shown on this statement in about...	And you will end up paying on estimted total of...
Only the minimum payment	3 years	$1,100

If you would like information about credit counseling services, call 1-800-123-4567.

REWARDS

Cashback Bonus		Anniversary Month May
(G)		
Opening Balance	$	11.69
New Cashback Bonus This Period		
Everywhere Else	+ $	0.01
Redeemed This Period	- $	0.00
Cashback Bonus Balance	$	11.70

To learn more, log in at YourBank.com

(A) Statement Header: This section shows the company name/logo, your account number, and the current statement's open and close dates.

(B) Current Account Summary: This includes the balance reported on your last statement, any payments and credits (which lower your balance), purchases made (which increase your balance), balance transfers from other accounts, cash advances taken from the credit account, bank fees, and interest charged. The new balance for the current statement period is totaled at the bottom.

(C) Payment Information: This is the current statement balance or the total amount from the account summary breakdown.

(D) New Balance: This is the total statement balance reported on your credit report. To avoid additional interest charges, you must pay your total statement balance in full.

(E) Payment Due Date: This is the last day possible to pay your MINIMUM payment to avoid late fees and negative marks.

(F) Late Payment/Minimum Payment Warning: Every statement includes these disclaimers to inform cardholders of the impact of only making minimum payments or paying late.

(G) Rewards: This is your summary of rewards for cash back or points.

(H) Credit Score: Some credit cards statements provide cardholders with their latest credit score.

Credit Card FAQs

Is it true that paying your credit card twice a month boosts your credit and shows the bank you are responsible?

No. It is a myth that paying your credit card twice a month boosts your credit. The bank is only required to report on-time (or late) payments and the total balance. You can pay on your credit card multiple times a month, but the amount paid is more important than the number of payments made.

When is the best time to pay your credit card each month?

The best time to pay your credit card is 2-3 days before the payment due date. This ensures all funds are processed before any late fees can be applied to your account.

How is my credit limit determined?

Your credit limit is determined by evaluating factors like your credit score, payment history, income, credit utilization, and large expenses

What is a balance transfer? Are they bad?

A balance transfer happens when you move your credit card balance from one bank to another for a small fee. Some issuers give cardholders lower interest rates with balance transfers. They are great when used strategically to help pay down credit card debt.

I was declined for a credit card. What should I do?

Consider starting with a secured credit card instead. Secured credit cards require a small (refundable) security deposit from the cardholder that you can use as your credit limit. This helps new credit card holders learn how to use their credit cards safely to build up good habits.

Do I really need to have a credit card in my money system?

No. Credit cards are not required to be a part of your money system. If you are uncomfortable with them or do not feel you are responsible enough, you can still build a strong money system and credit score without credit cards.

Credit Card FAQs

Should I hold a balance on my credit card?

If you have the money to pay your credit card statement off in full before the payment due date, pay it off. Do not hold a balance on your credit card from a previous month unless you absolutely cannot afford a full payoff. When you hold a balance, you incur interest (not the good kind), and you start digging your credit card debt hole.

Is it bad to close a credit card account?

Closing is a double-edged sword. it can improve your money system if the card you are closing is not helpful. However, your credit score can take a small hit. But this can be a minor setback for a maior comeback

Is there a limit to how many credit cards I can have? How many credit cards should I have?

Technically there is no specific limit to how many credit cards a person can have. However, a responsible credit card user should never have more credit cards than they can effectively manage. Less is more when it comes to credit card management.

Decision Tree: Should You Use Your Credit Card?

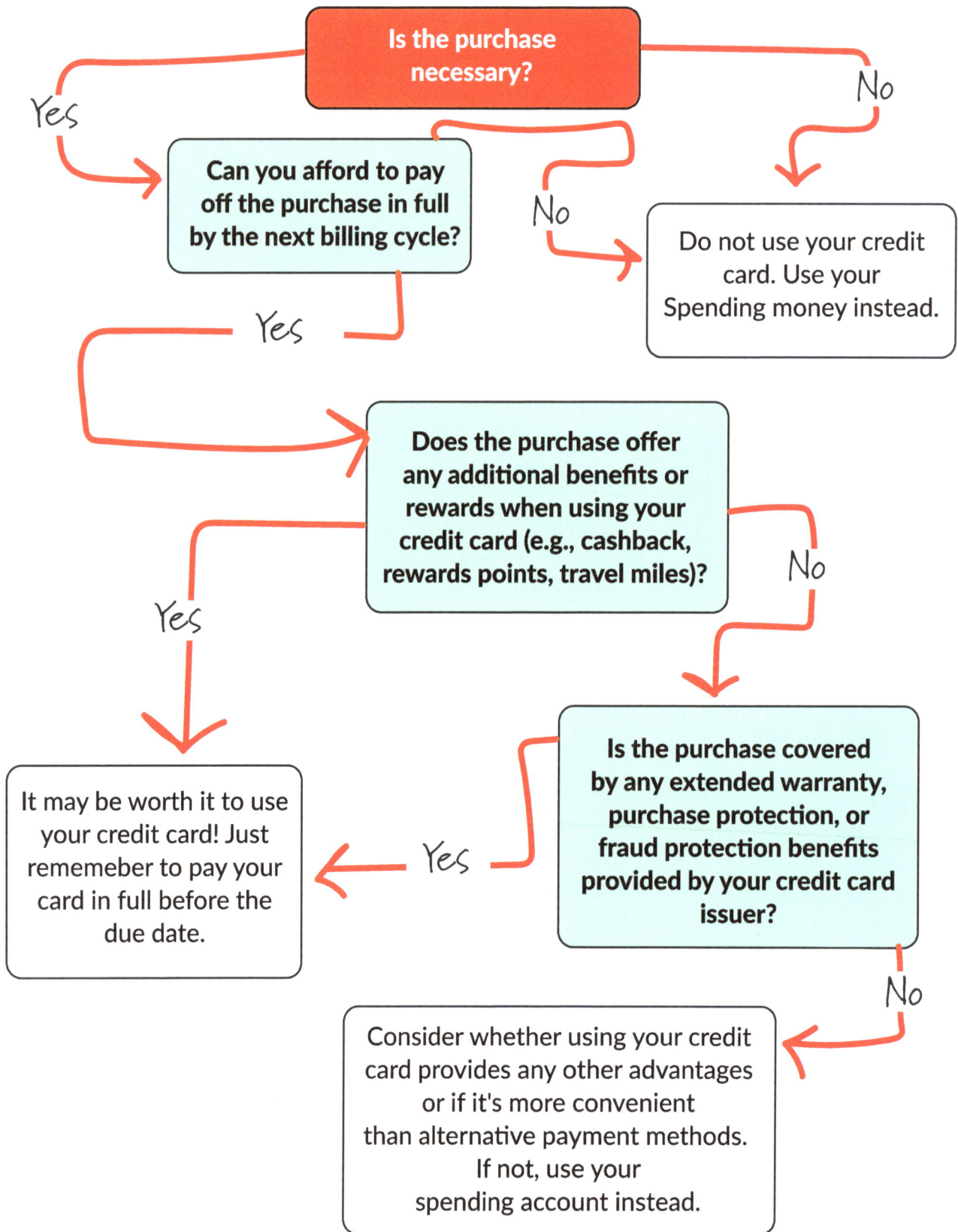

Is the purchase necessary?

Yes →

Can you afford to pay off the purchase in full by the next billing cycle?

No →

No →

Do not use your credit card. Use your Spending money instead.

Yes →

Does the purchase offer any additional benefits or rewards when using your credit card (e.g., cashback, rewards points, travel miles)?

Yes ↓

No ↓

It may be worth it to use your credit card! Just rememeber to pay your card in full before the due date.

Is the purchase covered by any extended warranty, purchase protection, or fraud protection benefits provided by your credit card issuer?

← Yes

No →

Consider whether using your credit card provides any other advantages or if it's more convenient than alternative payment methods. If not, use your spending account instead.

Rewards, Benefits, and Annual Fees

Which do you prefer, cashback or points? This is a hard question for some people. These reward systems are built into your credit card to provide cardholders with incentives to use their card. Cashback and points (flight, hotel, or general) are the most common reward systems. Everyone has a preference, but it's important to give your credit card a job. Be sure to read about the reward system for your card when you're approved. Your monthly statement will outline any earned rewards and a total reward balance.

Rich Tip: Keep an eye on your email inbox for any changes in rewards or benefits and take advantage of limited-time offers and perks by frequently checking your credit card's online portal.

With great credit cards come great fees. While many credit cards offer benefits to cardholders for free, some require annual fees to become a member. Annual fees can range from $39 to $695+ depending on the card level you're approved for. These annual fees are used to cover the costs associated with maintaining the card's benefits and services. This includes:

- Customer support
- Fraud protection
- Rewards programs
- Operational expenses

Credit Utilization

Your credit utilization is one of the most important things to pay attention to when using credit cards. Credit utilization refers to the ratio of the amount of credit you currently use compared to the total amount of credit available to you. The lower your credit utilization ratio, the better. High credit utilization suggests that you may be overextended financially and may have difficulty managing additional debt, which can negatively impact future accounts and borrowing. Lenders often prefer borrowers with lower credit utilization ratios because they are seen as less risky. Typically, a credit utilization of less than 30% is the best practice to maintain a healthy credit score. When your credit utilization is over 35%, your credit score may begin to be negatively affected. My suggestion is to aim to keep your credit utilization under 20% to be safe. You can set up a notification to warn you when you get close or go over the safe limit.

Determining Credit Utilization: $2,800 (total statement balance) / $8,000 (total credit limit)
= 35% credit utilization

Determing Safe Spending Limit: 20% (credit utilization) x $8,000 (total credit limit)
= $1,600 safe spending limit

Taking note of your statement end date is critical when trying to maintain a healthy credit utilization. Remember, the credit card company reports your balance to the credit bureaus once a month. When they report your balance, it's based on the amount reflected on your statement's end date. Take the extra step to make a payment on your credit card 2–3 days before the statement end date to ensure your total credit used is less than 20% of the credit limit for reporting purposes. After the statement closes, pay the remaining balance in full before the payment due date. This ensures you avoid paying interest.

Credit Cards for Everyday Use

Reflect on the past 12 months and ask yourself these three questions to determine if you should be using credit cards for everyday spending:

1. Do have current credit card balances from previous months?
2. Have you paid any credit card late fees in the past 24 months?
3. Have you struggled with paying your total credit card balance in full at the end of the month?

If you answered "yes" to any of the questions above, you are not ready to use credit cards for everyday spending.

This is the hard truth. It takes discipline and a strategic money system to truly be ready for everyday credit card use. Many people talk about the benefits of using credit cards over debit cards, but don't fall into credit card debt chasing cashback or reward points.

Before using your credit card for everyday spending, you should be able to confidently answer those questions with a strong "No".

Whether you're using credit cards for specific purchases or everyday items, you need to have spending rules. These rules are similar to your no-no list but are specifically for how you use your credit cards.

Act Rich, Be Responsible

EXERCISE #23:
Spending No-No List

Instructions:

Reflect on your current spending (exercise #8) and take note of the places where you spend most. In the space below write 1-2 new spending rules to keep you on track and give your credit cards a job.

- No using credit cards to purchase clothes, use spending account only!

Credit Card Everyday Spending Checklist

Before you get the card

☑ Review your current spending habits and take note of where you spend the most monthly

☑ Research credit cards that provide the highest rewards for your top three spending categories

☑ Select and apply to the best credit card based on your research

After you get the card

☑ Lock your debit card (digitally and physically), commit to only using your credit card, and never use both forms of payment at the same time

☑ Use your credit card for everyday expenses

☑ Pay your total credit card balance with your spending account funds

Credit Card Money System

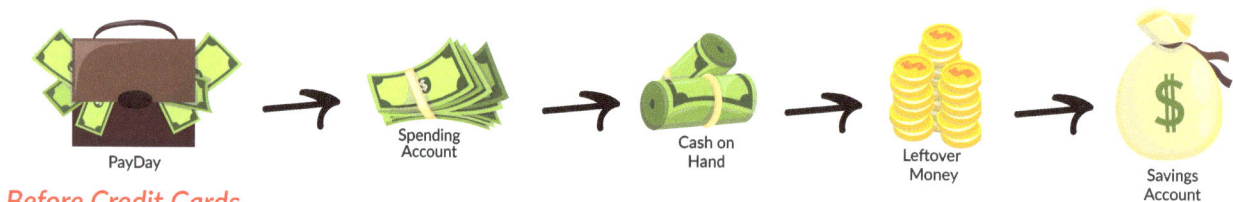

PayDay → Spending Account → Cash on Hand → Leftover Money → Savings Account

Before Credit Cards

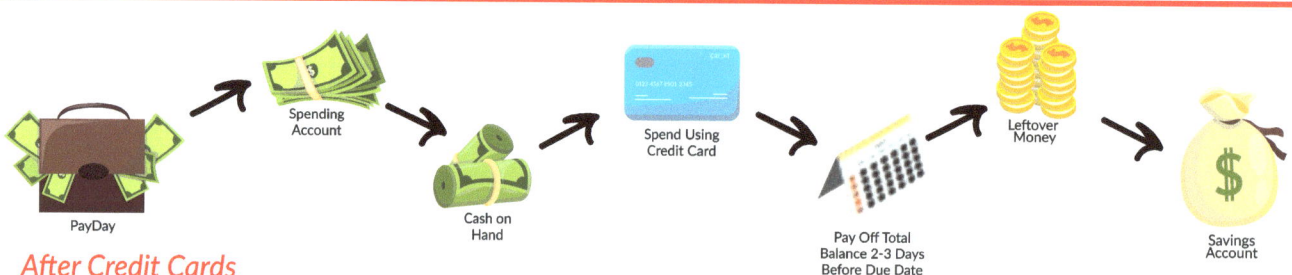

PayDay → Spending Account → Cash on Hand → Spend Using Credit Card → Pay Off Total Balance 2-3 Days Before Due Date → Leftover Money → Savings Account

After Credit Cards

Things to Avoid

Interest and late fees are the biggest things to avoid when using your credit card. The way to skip out on paying your credit card company interest and fees is to pay in full and on time every month. I know this is easier said than done, but it truly is the only way. A responsible credit card user can swipe their card all month long and pay $0 in interest and fees.

If you don't have enough money to cover your total statement balance, you will be charged interest. However, most people incorrectly understand the monthly interest charged to their accounts. The A in APR stands for ANNUAL. If your credit card APR is 24.99%, the credit card company divides this by twelve months to determine your monthly interest charge. For this example, the monthly interest rate would be 2.8%. This interest compounds monthly, which means the amount you owe to the credit card company will continue to increase when the balance is not paid in full. Credit card debt is a slippery slope that many of us experience, but there is always a way to climb out of it.

Rich Tip: Avoid DOUBLE DIPPING! If you're going to use your credit card daily, you should not use your debit card. This disrupts the money system and makes it challenging to track how much money is going out. Choose one method and stick to it.

Store cards may seem like a great idea when you're at the cash register of your favorite store, but the discount is rarely worth it. My first credit card was from a very popular panty store that will not be named. It was also how I learned the hard way that payment due dates are serious business. Store credit cards don't typically provide the same benefits and flexibility as credit cards from financial companies. The only benefit of using a store credit card is discounts when you shop at that specific store more.

The last trap you want to avoid is cash advances. Cash advances are offered by credit card companies, allowing cardholders to withdraw cash from an ATM or bank branch. When a person makes a cash advance, they're essentially borrowing cash against their credit limit instead of making a purchase. There are high fees associated with cash advances and little to no grace period. Unlike making regular purchases, cash advances start accruing interest daily until paid back in full, so it's best to avoid cash advances altogether.

Buy Now, Pay Later

Buy Now, Pay Later (BNPL) is everywhere. If you haven't heard of these new apps, here's the quick and dirty. You make a purchase using the app, but instead of paying the full amount upfront, you split it into installments to pay over time. It's a modern twist on layaway, but instead of waiting until you pay off the whole balance, you get your purchase immediately. What started for online fashion purchases has quickly grown to change how many people buy both in-store and online. Today, you can use BNPL for physical items and services across industries.

BNPL can be a game-changer when used strategically. Let's say you spot a great deal on a high-ticket item like a new laptop or a piece of furniture. Instead of paying for it all upfront, you could use BNPL to split the cost into manageable installments. This way, you can take advantage of the deal without draining your bank account all at once. Additionally, these apps can be handy for budgeting purposes. Say you have a tight month financially, but you need to replace your broken phone. By using a BNPL option, you can get the phone you need and spread out the payments over the next few months, making it easier to handle your expenses without feeling overwhelmed. This can also help you avoid dipping into your emergency fund. These apps can offer flexibility and convenience while helping you stay within your budget.

The best way to manage your BNPL charges is to create rules and boundaries. Some friends limit how many active payments they have at once. Other friends focus on when they buy items to ensure that the billing cycle syncs up with their paydays. Intentional spending should still be the goal when using BNPL apps because they're also part of your money system.

While BNPL can offer convenience and flexibility, users should also be aware of potential pitfalls. One major concern is overspending. Since these apps allow you to defer payments, it can be tempting to buy more than you can afford at the moment, leading to debt accumulation. Additionally, missing payments can result in late fees and potentially harm your credit score. Since these apps often don't require a credit check upfront, it's easy to overlook the fact that you're essentially taking on debt that needs to be repaid. Moreover, relying too heavily on these apps could mask underlying financial issues and hinder long-term financial plans.

I don't have a strong opinion on whether BNPL is "bad" or "good". However, I will say that it needs to be used strategically. If you're going to use these apps, it needs to make sense. If you can't find a strategic or sensible reason to add BNPL into your money system, it may not be worth the hassle. Harmful apps have no place in your new money system, so if your BNPL habits have negatively impacted your money, it's time to let it go.

Act Rich, Be Responsible

EXERCISE #24: Credit Card List

Instructions:

In the exercise below, list out all current credits. Be sure to include all the necessary information to have an accurate list of credit cards. The first one is done for you.

Card Name	Spending Purpose	Total Balance	Statement Balance	Statement Close Date	Due Date	Credit Limit	Interest Rate (APR)
Bank XYZ	Travel Spending	$2,234	$2,234	6th of the month	2nd of the month	$11,200	$19.99%
Bank 123	Gas & Groceries	$224	$324	20th of the month	17th of the month	$2,000	$24.99%

Section Key Points

- You should be intentional with your spending and create an allowance that gives you the ability to still have fun with your money.

- Create boundaries for your spending and money system. For every NO to a bad habit, there is a YES to a good habit.

- Credit cards are an open-book test; this is your chance to show the bank how responsible you are.

- BNPL can be helpful when used strategically; there's no shame in using them.

List five ways you will commit to being more intentional with your spending for the next three months.

How do you feel about your current spending habits? What difference would you like to see in the next three months?

Section Notes

REVIEW AND ADJUST YOUR FLEXIBLE BUDGET™

SECTION OBJECTIVES

1. Highlight the significance of conducting regular financial reviews to ensure your budget aligns with your lifestyle and habits.

2. Equip you with practical tools and techniques for evaluating your budget's performance.

3. Identify areas that require modification so you can prioritize financial goals and make informed decisions about reallocating resources.

WHY SHOULD YOU CARE?

Financial Flexibility: Identifying areas where you can cut back or reallocate funds ensures that your budget remains relevant and effective, helping you stay on track and avoid unnecessary financial stress.

Goal Tracking: Revisiting your budget regularly ensures that you're allocating resources in a way that maximizes progress toward your goals.

Maintain a Healthy Money System: Gathering your personal finance data will enhance your financial journey and encourage you to reward yourself for the hard work you've put into your finances.

Review and Adjust

Your budget is a living, breathing thing. It needs to continuously grow and evolve with you and your lifestyle. Here's something most budgeting experts won't tell you: the first month of a new budget will suck. The second month of a new budget will suck (just a little less). The third month of a new budget, it's a 50/50 toss-up.

Being uncomfortable while trying something new is normal. The thing is, you won't have enough data to know what's working and what needs to change until month three of your new budgeting strategy. Data exposes your habits and ultimately tells you what's working and what's trash. With good budgeting data comes good decisions on how to adjust your strategy to move closer to your vision of success.

Do you need to increase your income? Do you need to try using cash only for your spending money? Is your budget getting you closer to achieving your budgeting goals? What about your budget feels good?

Rich Tip:

Ask yourself these review questions every quarter:

1. What do I love about my budget?
2. What worked well this quarter?
3. What do I hate about my budget?
4. What didn't work well this quarter?
5. What can I do to get closer to my money goals?

Money Dates

Let's go on a money date! Don't worry; you don't have to have a romantic partner to go on this date. In fact, this date is strictly between you and your money.

People always ask, "How often should I review my budget?" The best answer to this question is, "Whenever you get paid." This is an easy rhythm that anyone can follow because, let's be real, we always know when payday is.

All money dates are not created equally. Some parts of your money system need more frequent reviews than others. Let's take a look into what needs to be reviewed and how often.

Money Date Checklist

ONE TIME EVENT

☐ *Set a date, time, and place:* This is a money DATE. Would you accept a first date without knowing what date, time, and place to show up? Your relationship with money is a lifelong commitment, and you need to treat it as such. Set a reminder in your calendar that includes where your money date will take place. This is a small brain hack to signal that it's a serious event.

EVERY MONEY DATE

☐ *Review your income:* Step One of the Flexible Budget™ (page 55) framework is reviewing your income. When on your money date, you need to check not only your deposited income but also your pay stub. Confirm that all deductions, exemptions, and taxes are correctly stated. Pay attention to deposit dates, hours worked, and paid time off. Should there be any major discrepancies, contact your employer immediately. You want to pay extra attention to these factors when you're starting a new job or promotional role.

☐ *Review your expenses*: Step Two of the Flexible Budget™ (page 66) is reviewing your expenses. When reviewing your autopay expenses, always confirm the dates and total amounts. Bills should not be a surprise, and there should be a record of payment for all expenses. For those bills you need to pay manually, ensure you have enough money in your bill pay account to cover the total. If there are any unexpected changes in expenses, don't be afraid to call your service provider for clarity or to dispute the charges. Lastly, when it comes to subscriptions, cancel anything that you haven't used within the last three months.

☐ *Review your debt:* If you don't have debt, then you can skip this step. The following are considered debt: auto loans, student loans, mortgages, personal loans, credit cards, buy-now-pay-later services, and any money you owe to other people or creditors. During your review, ensure that you know your due dates, minimum payments required, interest rate, and payoff total, and have a record of your last payment. Making a debt freedom/management plan is a critical part of your financial wellness journey.

☐ *Review your goals:* It should be noted that goals are not a one-and-done thing. Once you set your money goals, it's important to remind yourself of these goals every money date. Keeping your goals top of mind helps you visualize your success. Review your goals to stay the course and give yourself a morale boost. Evaluate if your goals still align with your definition of success, and if they no longer align, you have my full support and permission to refresh your goals.

☐ *Update your goal trackers:* As you learned in the Sticky Goals section (page 22), the "M" in SMARTY stands for measurable. For every sticky goal, there must be a way to track your progress. There are many different ways to automate your trackers, especially if you're using a budgeting app. If your progress tracker is automated, you should still manually review your progress to remind yourself of how well you're doing. Reviewing your trackers also motivates you to keep working toward success.

☐ *What's Working? What's Trash?:* There are two things your money date will uncover: what's working in your money system and what's trash. The objective is to keep doing all the things that are working and dump everything that's trash. Every money date, answer these two questions.

NOT SO FREQUENT

☐ *Review other money things:* Not every part of your money system requires constant monitoring. While it's important to track your money system closely, trying to make everything a priority can be overwhelming, and when you're overwhelmed with your money, the excitement is lost. While everything can't be a priority, remember to keep these categories in mind and set a review frequency since they're still part of your money system:

Credit score: Your credit score fluctuates throughout the month, but if you're not planning on opening a new line of credit in the next 6–12 months, you can get by reviewing it once every 1–3 months.

Investments: If you're a long-term investor, your portfolio will not require a lot of review. Monthly check-ins are perfect for individual brokerage accounts, but the frequency can increase depending on how often you buy shares.

Corporate benefits: Employer-related retirement accounts and other benefits can be monitored at a much lower frequency; review these accounts on a quarterly basis.

Personal information and beneficiaries: Your personal information and beneficiaries should be reviewed on an annual basis or whenever you have a major life event (e.g. marriage, birth, death).

Reward Yourself. Every successful money date deserves a reward. Positive reinforcement encourages you to keep going! The reward can be big or small, but make sure it is something that gets you excited and exclusive only to your money dates. It can be getting ice cream, watching your favorite TV show, having a glass of wine, or coloring in a coloring book after you finish your money date. No matter how you choose to reward yourself, remember, it is a requirement.

Lifestyle Creep

The last thing we need to discuss in this section is lifestyle creep. In short, lifestyle creep is the unconscious practice of slowly upgrading your lifestyle along with your income. This looks like changing your basic necessities like home, car, or food expenses with every promotion and pay increase. It's exciting to finally be able to afford luxury items and living, but lifestyle creep eats away at your ability to save and invest.

A good practice is to upgrade something major every 3–5 years (e.g., car, home, fun spending). Keeping your expenses the same while increasing your salary will help you avoid lifestyle creep and increase your disposable income. Otherwise, you might find yourself being a high earner who's still financially overwhelmed, and what's the point of having money if you still feel broke?

Flexible Budget™ Review Example

What you thought you would spend

What you actually spent

Category	Monthly Budget	Monthly Actuals
Gas/ transportation	100	72.39
Groceries	150	144.96
Cash on hand	40	40
Spending	184.16	158.43
Investing	391.27	391.27

Total money spent this month

Total Money Spent

$ __ __ __ , 8 0 7 . 0 5

Flexible Budget™ Review

Flexible Budget™ Review Example

Calculated in Step 4

Spending Allowance $ [ ][ ]2,265.43

SUBTRACT

Total money spent this month

Total Money Spent $ [ ][ ]1,400.00

EQUALS

Leftover money to be added to savings

Leftover Spending Money $ [ ][ ][ ],865.43

Act Rich, Be Responsible

Instructions:

In the table below, list your spending categories and the total monthly spending allowance originally budgeted in Step Four for each goal. Then, write your actual dollars spent in each category. Calculate the sum of your monthly actuals and fill in the spaces.

Category	Monthly Budget	Monthly Actuals

Total Money Spent $ _ _ _ , _ _ _ . _ _

Act Rich, Be Responsible

EXERCISE #26:
Flexible Budget™ Review

Instructions:

In the exercise below, write your total money spent. Then, write your spending allowance calculated in Step Four and calculate the total money left over by subtracting the total money spent from your spending allowance.

Spending Allowance $ ☐☐☐,☐☐☐.☐☐

SUBTRACT

Total Money Spent $ ☐☐☐,☐☐☐.☐☐

EQUALS

Leftover Spending Money $ ☐☐☐,☐☐☐.☐☐

Act Rich, Be Responsible

EXERCISE #27:
Money Date Checklist

Instructions:

Schedule a money date on your next payday. Write down your reward and follow the checklist to complete your money date reviews.

EVERY MONEY DATE

- ☐ Income Review
- ☐ Expense Review
- ☐ Debt Payment Review
- ☐ Update Goal Trackers

OPTIONAL REVIEWS

- ☐ Credit Score Review
- ☐ Investments Review
- ☐ Corporate Benefits Review
- ☐ Update Personal Information

What is working with my budget?

What is trash within my budget?

My money date reward is _____

Act Rich, Be Responsible

EXERCISE #28:
Quarterly Review

Instructions:

Answer the review questions below after three months of a new budget strategy.

What do I love about my budget?

What worked well this quarter?

What do I hate about my budget?

What didn't work well this quarter?

What can I do to get closer to my goals?

Section Key Points

- Give your new budgeting strategy at least THREE MONTHS before changing it.

- Money dates are a special time to get more comfortable with your personal finances.

- Always reward yourself. You deserve to celebrate yourself and your money.

- Lifestyle creep is a thief; do not let it steal your money.

List five ways to reward yourself after completing a Money Date.

Think about your past attempts at budgeting and financial management. What worked well? What was trash?

Section Notes

CHECK YOUR B.A.N.K™

SECTION OBJECTIVES

1. Learn to evaluate your needs, wants, and values before spending.

2. Learn to resist the temptation of impulse purchases.

3. Understand Check Your B.A.N.K™, an easy guide to making money moves.

WHY SHOULD YOU CARE?

Become More Intentional: Intentional spending empowers you to take control of your finances by eliminating wasteful expenses and aligning your spending with your desired life.

Priortize Yourself: When you spend with intention, you can prioritize the things that matter most to you, whether it's traveling, investing in education, or starting a business.

Promotes Money Positivity: Mindful spending positively impacts your financial health and overall well-being.

Making Money Moves

You have officially finished setting up your financial future, and I am so very proud of you. Let's not stop here, though. Before I leave you to handle your money on your own, I want to give you some guidance on how to make those real-life money decisions. This is where theory meets reality. You have all the tools to transform your money in theory, but this is real life, and real-life situations require real-life solutions.

Before you make a major money decision, I suggest you Check Your B.A.N.K™. This is the four-question checklist that will remind you to be intentional about your spending because trust me, things can (and will) get out of control if there's no intention, so let's Check Your B.A.N.K™ to make some powerful money moves.

BRING. What does this decision BRING to you? Think deeply about what this question is asking. Does this purchase bring you joy? Does it bring you peace? Does it bring you more time for the things you love to do? How does this decision add to your life? As far as I'm concerned, we only spend money for one of two reasons: to add joy or to stop pain. This reflection can also be reframed as, "What's in it for me?" What are you gaining from the money spent?

AFFORDABLE. Can I AFFORD this purchase? It's not just about the price tag. Think about your life and consider whether you can afford to shift your life and your future budget for this purchase. Consider not just the current sticker price but the maintenance and upkeep you'll have to pay moving forward. Take buying a new car, for instance. You can do the math, and it may seem like you can afford the $400 monthly payments, but that doesn't take into consideration the gas, insurance, garage fees, tags, mechanical maintenance, or car washes. So, before saying yes to a new purchase, remember today's yes can be tomorrow's "Oh, no!"

NOW. Do I need it NOW? Yes, time is of the essence, but it's also a made-up concept. Ask yourself, NOW or later? Most times, we look at something, think about it, and then realize the world will not come crashing down if we decide not to buy it right then and there. But there might be a special day when you're going through this checklist and realize, yes, I absolutely need to spend this money right now or else [insert the worst thing imaginable].

KNOCKOFF. Lastly, what is the cheaper KNOCKOFF alternative? Listen, nobody loves a good dupe like me. I remember the first knockoff Coach bag I bought. It was amazing. The bag was white with dark brown leather trimmings on it, and all the c's stitched into the fabric were different shades of pink and purple. I got it at the flea market, and nobody could tell me anything! Knockoffs got a rebrand, and we call them "dupes" now, but it's all the same. These are similar items that are up to 50% cheaper than buying directly from high-end stores. When you're considering your next money move, it's important to consider the alternatives before you spend your money. There will be times when you for sure want the real thing, and then there'll be other times when you're comfortable getting a knockoff. Whatever you choose, this is a reminder to consider all the available alternatives first.

Now that you have these four questions, you're ready to make your next money move. Let's see an example.

Check Your B.A.N.K™ Example #1

Should I move into a new apartment that costs $1,000 more than my current rent?

B - Bring. What does this decision BRING?

Reflect and ask yourself, what does this move bring? *Will it bring peace from something truly disturbing you? Will it bring some much-needed joy? What obstacles will it bring?* Don't only think about the positives; think about the negatives too. *Will this bring you less disposable income? Will it bring you maintenance expenses?* Think about all the things this decision will bring you.

What does this decision BRING?
I will be able to have more space for my office and move to a better neighborhood with a building that offers more amenities and security. I will have pay for the move and have a to consider finding more income opportunities to maintain my other living expenses.

A - Affordable. Can I AFFORD this move and rent increase?

Sometimes, we have the money to buy something but can't truly afford it. *What changes in your life and budget will you have to make to truly afford this purchase?* Consider the upkeep costs and the costs of changing your mind if you realize it wasn't the best decision. Remember, there are opportunity costs for everything. Maybe you can financially afford something, but you can't afford it physically, mentally, or emotionally. Reflect on the true affordability of this purchase.

Can I AFFORD this move and rent increase?
I can use my new office to build my side hustle and rent my space out for photoshoots. I will have to spend more on utilities and cleaning, but since I'll be closer to work, I'll pay less for gas. With my new promotion I will be bringing in $1,500 more every paycheck.

N - Now. Do I need to move NOW?

Do you need this purchase to happen now or later? We live in a digital age that profits off exclusivity, scarcity, and false urgency. Fear of missing out (FOMO) forces us to spend money unnecessarily. If you can't remember any of the other questions, keep this one at the top of your mind with everything you buy. *Do I need this now, or can it wait until later?* Timing is everything. While you can't predict the future, you can always ask, "Is this a purchase that truly needs to be made right now?"

Do I need this NOW or LATER?
My lease is up in three months, and I have to make this decision within the next 30 days.

K - Knockoff. What is the cheaper KNOCKOFF alternative?

Everybody loves a good dupe. Well, when I was growing up, the adults called them knockoffs. Whichever word you like to use, always look for cheaper alternatives and compare your options. Try to find a way to avoid paying the full price for anything. Find a coupon, get a discount, negotiate the deal, get something similar but different, and when all else fails, DIY. There are so many tools available for you to find similar but cheaper alternatives, so use them to your advantage. Don't listen to haters, and stop trying to keep up with influencers. If you want to buy the dupe because it works for you and your budget, do it! Compare alternatives and make the best money move for you.

What is the KNOCKOFF?
I could stay in my current apartment for another year or tour more apartments in the area to compare prices. I can also ask for any new resident discounts.

Check Your B.A.N.K™ Example #2

Should I buy a new $500 designer bag?

	What does this decision BRING?
B	Temporary happiness and a new item in my collection.

	Can I AFFORD this purchase?
A	I didn't plan for it, but I'll have enough money to buy it in just a month.

	Do I need this NOW or later?
N	I would like it now while it's on sale, but I can wait a month.

	What is the KNOCKOFF?
K	There are some Amazon dupes available for $50, but I really love the designer and want to opt out.

Act Rich, Be Responsible

EXERCISE #29:
Check Your B.A.N.K™

Instructions:

Answer the review questions below to intentionally think through your next money decision.

What do you want to spend money on?

What does this decision BRING?

Can I AFFORD this purchase?

Do I need this NOW?

What is the KNOCKOFF?

What do you want to spend money on?

What does this decision BRING?

B

Can I AFFORD this purchase?

A

Do I need this NOW?

N

What is the KNOCKOFF?

K

Section Key Points

- Always Check Your B.A.N.K™ before making a money decision.

- Intentional spending will be the difference between your financial success and your financial rock bottom.

- Nobody cares if you used a discount or a coupon for your purchases.

- Every decision is a money decision. Be intentional.

How do you define intentional spending?

Think about your last big purchase. How did the purchase make you feel? Are you still proud of that purchase? Would you make the same decision again?

Section Notes

CYBER-SECURITY FOR YOUR MONEY

SECTION OBJECTIVES

1. Learn more about FinTech hardware and software to understand how it impacts your money system.

2. Understand the risks cyber criminals pose to your personal finances.

3. Implement cybersecurity measures to safeguard your sensitive financial data, such as bank accounts and credit card details.

WHY SHOULD YOU CARE?

Direct Financial Impact: Cyberattacks can result in drained bank accounts, fraudulent credit card charges, and unauthorized access to investments, causing direct financial loss.

Identity Theft Consequences: A breach in personal finance cybersecurity can lead to identity theft, negatively impact your credit score, and cause long-term financial distress.

Privacy and Peace of Mind: Safeguarding financial information ensures personal privacy and peace of mind, allowing you to maintain control over your financial well-being.

How to Choose a FinTech App

We can't escape technology, no matter how hard we try. Money is digital just as much as it is physical. The FinTech industry is vast, and advancements in hardware and software have changed how we interact with money. One example of hardware updates would be the chips we now have in our banking cards, while software updates include anything from digital wallets to budgeting apps.

Breakdown of different FinTech Apps:

Online Banks (aka "Neobanks"): Online financial institutions. They typically offer better rates because they don't have the same expenses as a traditional bank.

Brick-and-Mortar Bank Apps: Apps presented by traditional banks to give customers mobile access to their accounts and services.

Financial Literacy Apps: Apps dedicated to educating users on the power of financial education.

Investing Apps: Where you go to make your money work for you, whether you're using a traditional brokerage, fractional shares app, or a robo investor.

Budgeting/Savings Apps: Apps designed to help you prioritize savings and budgeting as easily and efficiently as possible.

Peer-to-Peer Exchange: Apps that help users safely send money to others by connecting to existing bank accounts.

Virtual Wallets: Digital storage for your credit and debit cards, allowing you to easily make secure purchases online and in physical stores.

The magic of technology is that many apps can do more than just one of these actions. With that being said, it's important to limit how many FinTech apps you allow to access your personal information.

There are four questions you should ask yourself when you're researching a new FinTech app for your money system.

- What is missing from my money system?
- What problem was this app created to solve?
- Who is the creator of this app?
- How does this app make money?

What is missing from my money system? This workbook helps you answer this question. Technology is here to enhance what you've already created. When researching, think about your money goals and what can help you achieve them. Consider what's been a problem area for you in the past as well. Have you failed at tracking your expenses and need an app that's good at automatically organizing your budget? Are you forgetful and need an app to help you stay on top of due dates? Do you want to increase your net worth and need an app to help you better track your growth? Figure out what your money system is missing.

What problem was this app created to solve? Every app on the app store was created to solve a specific problem. Of course, apps can have many different capabilities, but they all have at least one core feature that makes them different. In your research, focus on understanding what problems the app was created to solve.

Who is the creator of this app? In modern times, transparency and diversity are key. There are many products that pretty much work the same. What can be a major differentiator, however, is the creator and mission of the company behind the product. You have the option to use apps created by people who look like you and care about the same causes you care about. If the creator of an app doesn't align with your values, then find one who does! Use your dollars to support founders working to create a world you want to see.

How does the app make money? This question is HUGE! Most people don't even consider how apps make money to operate, but friend, it truly is a big deal. Some apps aren't as transparent or as ethical as others. It's not a bad thing to pay for a financial app that helps improve your money system. Think about all the time and energy required to create an app. Money is needed for software development, user experience and design, customer service, marketing, and so much more. Apps are businesses that are ultimately in it for profit. If the consumers aren't paying for the platform directly, then they're paying indirectly. Apps are known to sell data, mislead consumers for in-app purchases, rely on affiliates with other products, and track consumer data to offer high-ticket products. Remember, "If the app is free, then you are the product."

Most of our lives include the internet. Money is digital, and it's your duty to protect yourself online. You don't have to be a cybersecurity expert to keep your dollars safe, but you do need to take potential security threats seriously. As the world becomes more digital, it's important to understand basic cybersecurity.

Email Addresses

The first line of defense in the digital world is your email address and password. Think of your email address as your unique identifier. Just like your other unique identifiers (home address, social security number, etc.), it should be protected and concealed from people who could potentially hurt you. Creating a separate email address, especially for your banking information, is a good way to protect your money and personal information. This email address should never be shared publicly or on any sites that aren't considered a part of your money system. Where you decide to host your email is also very important. While there are common free email hosting services, you might want to consider using an encrypted email address.

An encrypted email address employs encoding techniques to secure communication and protect sensitive information. Unlike regular email addresses, where messages are transmitted in plain text and can be intercepted or read by unauthorized parties, encrypted email addresses ensure that the contents of your emails remain confidential and inaccessible to everyone except you. This added layer of security safeguards personal and business communications, preventing potential data breaches, identity theft, and unauthorized access to your sensitive data.

Three Tips for a Secure Email Address

1. Avoid common or predictable patterns: Steer clear of using common phrases or patterns in your email address.

2. Opt for a secure email provider: Select a reputable and secure email provider that offers encryption, two-factor authentication, and strong privacy policies.

3. Use a mix of characters: Incorporate a mix of letters (both uppercase and lowercase), numbers, and special characters to make your email address more secure.

Passwords

Weak passwords pose significant security risks as they can be easily guessed or brute forced by attackers. Short, common, or dictionary-based passwords are vulnerable to password-cracking tools. Weak passwords grant unauthorized access to sensitive data, enabling identity theft, financial fraud, and privacy breaches. They compromise personal accounts, emails, and social media. To mitigate these dangers, you have to adopt strong, unique passwords and implement multi-factor authentication for enhanced protection.

PASSWORD BEST PRACTICES!

1. Length: Use passwords of at least 12 characters to increase complexity.

2. Complexity: Include uppercase and lowercase letters, numbers, and special characters (@, #, $, etc.).

3. Unpredictability: Avoid using easily guessable information like birthdates or common words.

4. Unique: Use different passwords for each account to prevent a single breach from compromising multiple accounts.

5. Avoid Personal Information: Don't use names, usernames, or easily accessible personal details in passwords.

6. Passphrases: Consider using random phrases or sentences to create strong yet memorable passwords.

7. Regular Updates: Change passwords periodically to maintain security.

8. Two-Factor Authentication (2FA): Enable 2FA whenever possible for an extra layer of protection.

9. Password Manager: Use a reputable password manager to generate, store, and manage complex passwords securely.

10. Educate: Regularly educate users about password security and the importance of following these best practices.

Password Managers

Password managers are essential tools for your online security. They offer a secure and convenient way to store, generate, and manage passwords. Using the same password across platforms can lead to devastating breaches if one account is compromised. Password managers create strong and unique passwords for each account and encrypt them, safeguarding your sensitive information from hackers.

They eliminate the need to remember multiple complex passwords, streamlining your digital life. Plus, they usually provide features like auto-fill and two-factor authentication. Using a password manager minimizes the risk of falling victim to phishing attacks, data breaches, and identity theft. It's a proactive step to fortify your online presence and ensure your personal information remains safe.

Two-Factor Authentication (2FA)

Two-factor authentication (2FA) is a security mechanism designed to add an extra layer of protection for online accounts and systems. It addresses the vulnerabilities of single-factor authentication by requiring you to provide two different forms of verification before logging into your account.

The two factors typically fall into one of three categories:

- Something you know (password)
- Something you have (a physical device or token)
- Something you are (biometric data like fingerprint or facial recognition).

By combining these factors, 2FA significantly enhances security, making it more difficult for unauthorized individuals to breach your account. When a user attempts to log in, they must first enter their password and then provide the second form of authentication, which could be a code sent to their phone or generated by an authentication app.

Enabling 2FA for financial accounts is critical due to the sensitive nature of the information they hold. Financial institutions often store personal data, credit card details, and transaction history, making them prime targets for cybercriminals.

To set up 2FA for financial accounts, log in to your account settings and navigate to the security section. From there, you can choose your preferred 2FA method and receive a one-time code via text, email, or an authentication app. Some financial institutions might offer additional options, such as biometric verification (i.e., FaceID or TouchID).

Authentication apps, such as Google Authenticator, Authy, or Microsoft Authenticator, generate time-based codes that change every 30 seconds. These apps are considered more secure than text messages because they work offline and are less susceptible to SIM-swapping attacks. They also offer the convenience of generating codes even when the device isn't connected to the internet. Text message verification, on the other hand, sends a one-time code to the user's registered phone number, which they then input to complete the authentication process. While convenient, cybercriminals can intercept text messages through techniques like SIM card cloning or social engineering, making them less secure than authentication apps, so it's best to use authentication apps whenever possible.

Social Media

Social media has become an integral part of our lives, allowing us to connect, share, and express ourselves. However, the allure of sharing personal information can lead to oversharing, which can have major consequences. Oversharing refers to revealing excessive personal details online, such as your location, daily routines, financial information, etc. Unfortunately, cybercriminals and malicious actors can exploit this information for identity theft.

Every social media platform offers different privacy settings to control who can access and interact with your content. Regularly reviewing and updating these settings is essential to ensure your safety. Limiting the visibility of your posts to close friends, using strong and unique passwords, and enabling 2FA are other simple yet effective ways to enhance your account security. Also, please be careful about accepting friend requests from strangers, as this can give them access to your personal information. Protect your financial data just as much as you work to protect your social media accounts. Not so fun fact, going viral on social media can be a huge security risk, be sure to monitor what information you share online in public forums.

Scammers and Hackers

Scams are at an all-time high, threatening your personal and financial security. Awareness of common online scams is the first line of defense. "Phishing" is a big one. This happens when cybercriminals impersonate legitimate institutions through emails, text messages, or websites to trick people into sharing sensitive information. Other common scams include offers that seem too good to be true (e.g., fake lottery wins or unrealistically cheap products), tech support scammers who pretend to be from reputable tech companies to gain access to personal information, and phone scams. Recognizing these tactics empowers you to steer clear of potential threats.

Phishing attempts often rely on psychological manipulation and urgency to bypass your rational thinking. Safeguarding against these attacks requires a cautious approach. Firstly, verify the sender's legitimacy before clicking on any links or sharing information. Hovering over links to reveal their actual destinations and cross-checking email addresses can help unveil potential scams. Secondly, be wary of unsolicited communications that evoke emotions such as fear or excitement, as scammers frequently exploit these emotions. Staying informed about new phishing tactics helps you avoid falling into these traps.

When faced with a suspected scam, it's essential to take prompt action. Reporting scams not only protects you but also helps prevent others from becoming victims. Most legitimate companies and organizations have channels for reporting scams, which can include forwarding suspicious emails to designated addresses.

In the case of financial scams, immediately contacting your bank or credit card provider can halt unauthorized transactions. If personal information has been compromised, it's best you closely monitor your accounts and place fraud alerts on your credit reports. If the scammers call your phone, hang up and call your bank. Furthermore, sharing your experiences and warning friends and family about scams can create a network of awareness and deter potential scammers.

Online Transactions Safety

Safeguarding financial transactions and personal information in the digital age requires a combination of awareness, proactive measures, and cautious decision-making. By following best practices for online banking and financial app safety, securing credit card information, and shopping safely online, you can significantly reduce the risks associated with cyber threats and fraud. Maintaining a secure digital environment for financial transactions and personal data is a shared responsibility between you and your service providers.

Protecting your credit card information is essential in a world where digital transactions have become the norm, so always verify the legitimacy of websites before entering your credit card details. You can do this by looking for "https" in the website's URL. This indicates a secure connection and will help you avoid making purchases on unsecured or suspicious sites.

Before making a purchase:

1. Verify the credibility of the online store.

2. Read reviews, check for contact information, and ensure the website has a secure checkout process.

3. Avoid clicking on suspicious links or pop-up ads, as they might lead to phishing sites aiming to steal personal information.

4. Ensure the website's URL begins with "https://" and displays a padlock symbol.

Act Rich, Be Responsible

EXERCISE #30:
Cybersecurity Checklist

Instructions:

You can use this checklist to protect your money before a cybersecurity attack.

One-Time Check

○ Turn on banking notifications

○ Enable two-factor authentication (2FA) for financial accounts

○ Choose a password manager

○ Review and adjust privacy settings on all social media accounts

○ Unfollow and remove any suspicious accounts

○ Review, unsubscribe, and delete any old accounts or profiles

○ Create a separate email address for your financial accounts

○ Remove saved credit/debit card information from shopping sites

○ Set up automatic updates for operating systems and software apps

---

Routine System Check

○ Regularly review your online presence and perform necessary cleanups

○ Review your bank and credit card statements monthly

○ Back up financial data to an external drive or secure cloud storage

○ Use credit cards or secure payment methods for online purchases

○ Monitor your credit report regularly for any suspicious activity

○ Update all passwords with a unique combination of letters, numbers, and special characters

○ Report and block suspected phishing emails or messages

Immediately report if you are the victim of identity thief to the Federal Trade Commission, your local police department, your bank, and credit reporting agencies.

Section Key Points

- If the app is FREE, then YOU are the product. Always do your due diligence to find out how an app makes money.

- Research your FinTech apps FIRST! Ask the right questions to create a plan to use technology to make your money system even better.

- Utilize multiple security layers such as strong passwords, two-factor authentication, and encryptio to create a shield against cyber threats.

- Routinely monitor your bank statements, credit reports, and investment portfolios for suspicious activity.

Reflect on your current habits and identify areas where you can enhance cybersecurity measures to protect your financial assets.

Do you have a plan in place to respond to potential cyber threats or financial breaches? If not, what steps can you take to prepare?

Section Notes

FINAL MONEY THOUGHTS

Money shouldn't be confusing or overwhelming. It's my hope that since reading this workbook, you have a clear guide on how to be financially responsible without sacrificing fun in your 20's. I am over the moon that you chose me as a trusted guide in this chapter of your money journey. I do not take this honor lightly.

NOW THAT YOU'VE COMPLETED THIS WORKBOOK, YOU CAN:

- Stop being afraid to check your accounts.

- Get serious about saving.

- Visually see how your money is moving.

- Start creating your best life.

This was all the work you needed to do to get build a strong financial foundation. There's no turning back now! You have started a new chapter in your money story, and this workbook is the blueprint. I'm happy that I could help you get started. The hardest part is over; now, all you need to do is reward yourself for this major accomplishment.

As a reminder, friend, this is just the beginning of what you can achieve financially. With this strong foundation you will be able to level up your finances in so many ways. Your financial future comes in levels. Your future can look however you want it to with enough money to do it. Financial freedom looks different on every person but you must master the basics before getting more complex. Soon you will be ready to make bigger investments, better donations, or travel the world in style. For now, just go make that money friend!

Final Self-Assessment

Your last exercise is a self-reflection one. Addressing your money means taking responsibility and giving yourself a good, hard look in the mirror. You have completed several financial exercises throughout this workbook and now it is time to take a final self assessment. After you have answered the following questions open and honestly compare your new assessment to your first assessment.

EXERCISE #31:
Self-Assessment

Instructions:

For each statement below, rate yourself on a scale of 1 to 10 (1 being completely disagree and 10 being completely agree) based on how much the statement reflects your current feelings. This will help you understand where your money mindset is today.

I feel confident in my ability to make strategic money decisions.

1   2   3   4   5   6   7   8   9   10

I feel confident in my ability to increase my current income.

1   2   3   4   5   6   7   8   9   10

I feel confident in my ability to manage the money I make.

1   2   3   4   5   6   7   8   9   10

I feel confident in my ability to achieve my current money goals.

1   2   3   4   5   6   7   8   9   10

I feel like I have a safe space to ask tough money questions.

1   2   3   4   5   6   7   8   9   10

I feel like I am financially responsible.

1   2   3   4   5   6   7   8   9   10

I feel confident in my power to change my current financial situation.

1   2   3   4   5   6   7   8   9   10

About the Author

Mykail James is a highly respected public speaker, financial educator, and content creator who's passionate about empowering young professionals to take control of their finances. With over a decade of experience in the financial industry, Mykail has a deep understanding of the money challenges and opportunities people face today. Through her online persona, "The Boujie Budgeter®," she breaks down complex money topics such as budgeting, investing, and credit, helping her community of over 70,000 Gen Z professionals develop the knowledge and skills they need to finance their best life and achieve their goals. With her dynamic speaking style, Mykail has a reputation for leaving audiences feeling entertained, motivated, and equipped with the tools they need to succeed.

Mykail's work is inspired by her own transition into Corporate America. Her firsthand experience makes her relatable to many recent graduates. Not only does she provide tangible action steps to obtaining financial stability, but she also helps her audience identify money trauma that may be blocking them from financial success.

Since beginning her career as a financial literacy educator and advocate in 2019, Mykail has worked with organizations such as the Howard University Trio Program and public schools within the District of Colombia, Maryland, and the Northern Virginia Metropolitan area. She has also worked with individuals, businesses, and non-profit organizations. Over the course of her professional career, she has curated workshops and interactive lectures to engage her audience and motivate them to make money moves.

Mykail is a first-generation college graduate from the Washington, DC area. She received both her Bachelor's and Master's in Business Administration with a concentration in accounting from Hampton University in Hampton, Virginia. Mykail is a Certified Financial Literacy Instructor through the National Financial Education Council. In 2018, she returned to the Washington, DC, metro area to pursue her dream of educating, motivating, and inspiring others to create the life they desire.

If you're looking for more ways to continue your money journey, here's how you can connect with me and find a community of other people just like you:

Get Access to Digital Resources

If you loved the resources provided in this book, grab your additional resources and copies at: https://moneyinyour20s.com/exercises

Join the Young, Rich, & Responsible® Community

Young, Rich, & Responsible® is the place for young professionals to grow financially, personally, and professionally. Join the community of young professionals and get valuable information tailored specifically for those just getting started in this thing called adulting.

https://www.moneyinyour20s.com

Invite me to your College or Corporation

If your last financial education workshop was a complete snoozefest, it's probably because you didn't invite me! Contact my team today at partnerships@boujiebudgets.com to schedule a financial literacy workshop that will have your students talking for years to come.

www.ingramcontent.com/pod-product-compliance
Lightning Source LLC
Chambersburg PA
CBHW050907210326
41597CB00002B/52